Fly Fishing
Small Streams

Fly Fishing
Small Streams

by John Gierach

Stackpole Books

Illustrated by Deborah Bond

Cover painting from the original oil "Stalking the
Brown" by Robert K. Abbett

Published by
STACKPOLE BOOKS
5067 Ritter Road
Mechanicsburg, PA 17055

Printed in the United States of America

10   9

Jacket and Book Design by Art Unlimited

LIBRARY OF CONGRESS
Library of Congress Cataloging-in-Publication Data

Gierach, John.
    Fly fishing small streams / by John Gierach; illustrated by Deborah Bond.
        p.   cm.
    ISBN 0-8117-2290-2
    1. Fly fishing.   2. Trout fishing.   I. Title.
SH451.G54   1989
799.1'755—dc19   88-16015
                                                                            CIP

To A. K. Best

Contents

A Finely Balanced Environment

The kind of fly fishing you like best has a lot to do with how you view the sport and how you'd like to see yourself: big-time sportsman, iron-jawed trophy hunter, contemplative backwoodsman—whatever. It's usually a pretty accurate view because it's not made consciously. Something looks neat, you try it, and, sure enough, it *is* neat. End of procedure. You may talk about it—especially with other fishermen—but it is not really open to serious discussion.

Many of us have elevated fly fishing (especially our favorite kind) to the highest category of human endeavor: something we don't have to explain unless we feel like it. Of course, if we *do* feel like explaining it, look out. We're liable to start referring to it as an "art" and maybe even sit down and write a book or something.

I'm like that with small trout streams. I did my first fly fishing on one (caught my very first trout on a fly and all that) and still think they give you the best of everything that fly fishing is about—trout, of course, being only one of many things. That's because I tend toward the contemplative backwoodsman self-image. You know, the solitary fisherman, man of few words, who fishes his secret spots and has the patience to rest a pool for three hours if that's what it takes.

Not that I'm really like that, but it doesn't hurt to

The North Fork of the St. Vrain: the archetypal small stream.

pretend.

I know what *I* mean when I say "small stream"—I can picture dozens of them—but this is probably a good place to try and come up with some kind of a real working definition of the term so we'll all know what we're talking about here.

The St. Vrain River, the main branch of which flows right across the road from the house here, is a perfect example. Don't let the word "river" fool you; it's just part of the name on the map and I'll have to admit it's a little overblown. Some people, when they've come up here to fish it for the first time, have looked at me and said, "You mean that's *it?*"

Some older maps call it the St. Vrain *Creek*, which is considerably more descriptive.

In the almost twenty years I've fished it I've somehow never gotten around to pacing off its width, but there is no place on it where you couldn't stand on one bank and comfortably roll-cast to the other, and you don't have to be a terribly hot roll caster, either. There are plenty of places to cross it in nothing more than hip boots and it is not navigable except by the occasional kid in an inner tube.

When the water is clear, which is most of the time, there's no place where you can't see the bottom, although in some spots it looks deliciously indistinct, mysterious and fishy, especially below the irrigation dams and under the bridges.

That's through most of the season, of course. In a wet year the spring runoff can turn it from a creek into a river for a few weeks with flows high enough to drown mule deer fawns who try to swim it, and attract the odd kayaker. Sometimes, fishing it in the weeks after the runoff has peaked, I've found the carcasses of deer, and once a crash helmet. The old-timers around here have even told of minor floods, and if you crawl under my house and look at the sandstone foundation where it hasn't been bleached by the sun, you can see the water-mark from the last one.

This is probably the single most worrisome part of living on a small trout stream. The occasional flood can be dangerous, and it's definitely unfishable, so let's not talk about it anymore.

Floods notwithstanding, let's say a small stream is one that you can cast across easily just about any-where on it, that you can wade—and often even cross—in hip boots, that is way too small for boats, and that has most of its structure pretty well exposed to view. For the purpose of this discussion, we'll also assume it has trout in it.

And that's as far as I plan to go by way of definition. I'm not even going to deal with the fact that what the people where you live call a "river" may turn into a small stream in the fall when the flow is down. I should also probably try to avoid the word "intimate," which has been overused, although that *does* describe what I have in mind.

To my eye, small streams are invariably pretty places. By nature, they're the tributaries of the larger rivers, the ones that attracted civilization in the first place and where the towns and cities now sit spoiling their an-cestral lifelines with pollution. The small streams (or creeks or brooks or whatever you want to call them) are in the headwaters, and these days that tends to be na-tional or state forest, national park, wilderness area, or some such thing. "Out in the country," in other words.

If the phrase "out in the country" doesn't get you at

least a little bit excited, you have picked up the wrong book. Put this one down and go get yourself a John Updike novel.

Small streams differ from rivers in a number of ways that are important to both trout and fishermen. They may both have the same kinds of structures—man-made and natural—but the small stream carries less water and that makes a big difference.

From the trout's point of view, the deep water of a big river means sanctuary. He can dart to it when threatened by his natural predators, he can lounge around down there in the winter when the water is cold (even by trout standards) and his own metabolism has slowed to the point of stasis (the fishy version of hibernation) and he's not as easily reached by fishermen.

The life of a river trout may not be what you'd call easy, but it's usually not too bad, either—all things considered.

Trout will often do well in small streams through the summer months, but the low winter flows can be deadly. Those deep, safe holes for wintering over just aren't there in many cases and, it probably goes without saying, big trout need deeper water to spend the winter in than little trout do. That, rather than food supply, is why some small streams just never grow big trout, or at least not very many of them.

I'm told by those who have done the studies that many small streams have plenty of fish food and would support larger trout if the fish had the habitat in which to wait out the winters. In just about every stream habitat improvement project I've seen, the idea was to deepen the water so the fish could hold over more successfully. On the ones that worked, most everything

else took care of itself, with no outside help from biologists or bulldozers.

I'm talking about freestone mountain creeks now,
the ones I've had the most experience with, but there
are exceptions—lots of them. Like spring creeks, for
instance. These things often qualify as "small streams"
in every way, but grow enormous trout on a regular
basis anyway. More on that later.

Food availability is the next major factor in the quality of a trout stream. More food equals bigger trout,
and the physical size of the stream in question is less
important than things like water chemistry, bottom
structure, bankside cover, types of vegetation, diversity
of insect species, and so on.

Traveling around as a tourist fisherman, you can get
it into your head that the big rivers are necessarily
more productive than the small streams, but that's a
kind of self-fulfilling prophecy. When you travel to fish,
you generally go to a good river, one that's known for
big trout and lots of them. Sure enough, there are a lot
of trout—and a lot of trout fishermen, too. The place
didn't get famous by accident.

But you can learn a lot by getting off on your own.
Just last summer, on a trip through northern Montana,
my friend Jim Pruett and I made a point of fishing the
Swan River, a real honest-to-god *river* that we had heard
absolutely nothing about except for vague allowances
that there were some trout in it.

You know what we thought. We figured we had a
sleeper, like in the old days: a Montana river full of fat,
wild, stupid trout that no one got around to fishing
because it was too far from West Yellowstone and all
those waters you read about in the magazines.

Not so. It was a big, pretty river all right, complete

with heart-attack-style wading and bottomless holes, but it held little more than the odd small fish. There just didn't seem to be much for them to eat: you could pick up a dozen rocks off the bottom before you'd find so much as a caddis larva.

The word locally was that there was a good run of Dolly Varden (otherwise known as bull trout) up it in early summer from Swan Lake, but that fishing for the resident trout was widely considered to be poor.

"Fly fishermen around here usually go down around Yellowstone," the guy said.

Live and learn. Total disappointment is rare on a fishing trip—especially one that is not over yet—but we *were* a little sorry to have left the small stream we'd been fishing the day before down in the Deer Lodge National Forest. The thing had been covered with caddis and mayflies, with big black stonefly nymphs under every rock. We'd caught much bigger trout there, and more of them.

That little stream, which our hosts had kindly led us to (we'd never even have known it was there otherwise) and asked us not to name publicly, was never more than six or eight yards wide and maybe waist to armpit deep in the best holes. It held cutthroat, brook trout, and some Dollys, with the occasional trout up to fifteen inches. Parts of it were public, and on some of the private stretches permission to fish was not impossible to get.

We fished it in chest waders because that's all we'd brought, but hip boots would have worked just fine and would have been a lot cooler, too.

It flowed through mixed ponderosa pine and fir country with lots of exposed boulders in the streamcut and a pretty steep gradient. It was cool, shady, verdant, and secret. At one point I remember hearing cars go by on the county road, but I couldn't see them. And they couldn't see me. When I sit back and think of a "small stream," in the dead of winter with a fire going in the stove and the block heater on the truck plugged in, that's what I see. Or what I see first, that is. Small streams are all small, but other than that they do what they like and the diversity is fabulous.

At the lower altitudes and on flatter ground, they tend to be placid and slow flowing, with wide bends. The bend pools may be deep and the banks may be undercut. An undercut is A-number-one trout habitat, never to be passed up.

Slower currents often mean more siltation on the stream bottom. This can cover over valuable rubble rock insect habitat and make for a marginal trout stream or provide a home for great herds of burrowing nymphs, depending, again, on a whole textbook full of environmental factors.

Tree-lined banks provide shade, and that's good because the water needs to be kept cool, and trout *like* shade. Fallen leaves also contribute to the decaying organic matter on the stream bottom that is the beginning of the food chain. On the nontechnical side, there are few places as cozy and secretive as a forest creek.

Maybe the stream runs through a meadow. That can be good, too. Meadows grow grasshoppers, and enough grasshoppers make for fat trout. The soft ground is also more easily undercut, and the casting is easier.

Some trout streams go into a transition stage at the lower altitudes. At some point the stream will go from cold-water aquatic insects and trout to warm-water bugs and maybe something like smallmouth bass or panfish. In ecology, transition zones where one habitat type shades into another are known for a greater than normal diversity of species: that is, lots of different bugs to be eaten by more than one kind of fish. Such places, if left to their own devices, can be terribly rich and healthy. It's not unusual for the best brown trout to be caught at that point on a small stream where you might also hook a smallmouth bass or a bluegill.

In steeper country the streams will typically be down in the canyons they've cut over more times than we're able to visualize. They'll have stayed narrow here and the gradient will be more severe. That means faster water where the pools and riffles will be smaller and closer together, sometimes even jumbled up together into pocket water. The shade of the canyon will keep the water cold and the riffles and plunges will keep it nicely aerated. The sound it makes—more than a babble but less than a roar—is just plain lovely.

Higher yet, a stream may flow through a mountain meadow or moraine, often with a canyon on either end, for a short stretch. Here the water is still cool and full of oxygen, but the current is slower and deeper, with cut banks, holes, logjams, and other structures that trout like. Free from the restraints of the canyons, the stream will wander around out in the open, making wide S curves with deep bend pools on the outside of each one.

Maybe there are some beaver ponds. These are usually found on fairly level stretches of stream (surprisingly short ones, at times) and can be very good news for fishermen.

Beaver Ponds

A new beaver pond, especially one on a very little creek with the smallest of trout in it, is the ultimate in

A beaver pond in the Rocky Mountains.

stream-improvement projects. You don't even have to cut a road to get the heavy equipment in. The beaver dam backs the stream up into a small lake. (I almost said "artificial lake," but it's not artificial at all, is it? It's perfectly natural.)

The water gets deeper, there's more of it in one spot, and it floods dry land, trees, and underbrush. The flooded stuff becomes cover and the increased amount of decaying organic matter makes the water richer. The aquatic insect population gets larger and the little trout that find themselves there eat the bugs and get bigger, too. The fish also stand a better chance of wintering over successfully in the deeper water.

It's perfect, for a while at least, and in the first few seasons of its life a beaver pond can grow trout that are much larger than what was there before. A further advantage is that new beaver ponds are usually not widely known. They can be hard to locate but, once found, they can be yours until the word spreads.

And remember, if you happen to stumble onto one, whether or not the word spreads is at least partly your responsibility.

Beaver ponds can really fix up the smallest of streams, those trickles that hold a few straggling, tiny trout that have worked up in there from downstream and who seem to be just realizing their mistake. Without beaver ponds, some little streams would be useless to all but the craziest of fly fishermen.

Lakes

Natural lakes also have a way of supercharging small feeders that, being too little to constitute year-round habitat and being way back in the woods as they are, would otherwise be pretty uninteresting. Even a fair-tomiddling-sized trout lake will sometimes pump surprisingly good trout into its feeders and may even provide spawning runs of fish at the right times of year.

It's been my experience that, during the prime fishing months, at least, the creeks are more regularly dependable than the lakes, with trout feeding through the day instead of just in the mornings and evenings. I've often ended up wandering around on a little feeder creek, catching trout during the day while the lake I came to fish is sitting back there doing its best impression of a fishless body of water.

Trout

I'm thinking here of places where the trout are wild—either native or the results of management programs where the idea was to establish breeding, self-sustaining populations of fish. When hatchery trout are stocked in a lake, they'll often just sit there patiently waiting to be caught and creeled before they starve to death or die of exposure. Running up the feeder creeks to explore or spawn is often just not on the agenda of most of these fish.

Granted, a percentage of the stockers will sometimes hold over for a season or more, and occasionally they'll even go wild to become what you'd have to call feral trout. That's something you can realistically hope for but it's not something you can count on.

I guess I share a prejudice with lots of other fly fishers in this area: I don't much care for hatchery trout. They're better than no trout at all, but otherwise they're inferior in every way to their wild relatives.

It's not so much that stockers are too easy to catch to be interesting, as some say. In fact, they can be damned difficult at times and, for that matter, wild trout can be disturbingly easy. But hatchery fish are, well . . . they're from a *hatchery*; they don't seem to belong in the stream, they're often of the wrong species (rainbows where cutthroats should live, for example), most are pale and sickly looking when compared to wild fish and, having been raised on Purina Trout Chow, they aren't very good to eat.

I know; it's not supposed to matter how good wild trout are to eat because you'll be releasing them. Fine, I usually do that, too. Still, the knowledge that if you did break down and eat one he'd be delicious adds a certain flavor to fishing for wild trout, so to speak.

Stockers also tend to be of uniform size, while wild fish hold that element of drama: there could always be a bigger one.

To be fair, I have to say that some wildlife agencies around the country strive to keep their hatchery fish in the best condition possible—often by introducing new strains as brood stock—but there are financial constraints on that and, after all, the whole idea behind this kind of fish culture is to raise trout that do well in concrete-sided hatcheries, not necessarily in wild streams. And, of course, the objective of most put-and-take stocking programs is the highest possible "return to creel" ratio. The quicker the fish go from stocking truck to stream to frying pan (or garbage can, as the case may be), the happier everyone is.

Hatchery trout strike me as being a lot like domestic turkeys: caricatures of the real thing. I once heard a turkey breeder say that the ideal bird would be featherless, skinless, boneless, gutless, and perfectly square.

One of the many advantages of small streams, especially the more remote ones, is that the trout in them are likely to be homegrown: that is, fairly wild, if not actually indigenous. In fact, some of the more obscure native subspecies we still have held out not in the big rivers and lakes they once inhabited, but in small streams back in the bushes where little or no stocking was ever done and where fishing pressure was light. For instance, the pretty little greenback cutthroat, once thought to be extinct, was rediscovered in the fifties in a tiny creek not far from here that had been all but forgotten by local fishermen because it was "too small to bother with."

It's rare these days to find a small stream holding trout that actually evolved in that very drainage, but little feeder creeks anywhere in the vicinity of trout country are likely to support fish. They're often the result of past plantings in the lakes and larger rivers in the neighborhood: trout that have wandered out into the small surrounding streams, taken up residence, and otherwise gone pretty much wild. In some instances they live largely undisturbed lives as the general crowd of fishermen work the rivers and hike the backcountry trails right to the headwater lakes, ignoring the creeks that connect the two.

Then again, sometimes you'll be fishing a river filled with something like browns or rainbows, only to wander half a mile up a little feeder to find cutthroats or maybe brook trout. If you have a romantic streak, as I do, you want to believe they've always been there, and maybe they have. More likely they came from backcountry stockings of different species or one of the programs designed to reintroduce native trout into areas where they had disappeared.

Sometimes it's not clear how they got there, and it becomes one of those sweet little guarded mysteries. "Don't tell anyone," you say to a friend, "but there are some brook trout up there." And if he actually *doesn't* tell anyone, then he really *is* your friend.

Fish Psychology

Whatever their pedigree happens to be, small-stream trout have a spooky streak, a propensity to bolt for cover at the slightest hint of anything weird. That, I think, is because they live their whole lives in what a lake or river fish would consider to be dangerously shallow water. If you're a bird-watcher, a small trout stream away from the traffic of fishermen is a good place to spot kingfishers perched on bare branches, herons carefully wading the shallows, or maybe ospreys gliding around in the sky. Just put a bookmark in your field guide at the fish-eating bird section.

I started to say that, shy or not, small-stream trout are also sort of raspy and aggressive, having the same kind of unpredictable split personalities some of us humans do—but that's not always true. It *is* true in most of the creeks I fish near home, which are freestone mountain streams where insects are not quite plentiful enough for the fish to have become spoiled and lazy. It's not that these creeks are exactly spartan, either, they're just not the mind-boggling bug factories that make for fly-fishing legends.

In that way I think they're typical of the majority of small trout streams around the country that are plenty good enough to grow trout, but that still fall short of what we like to call "blue ribbon" habitat. So maybe I'll stand by what I started to say, as long as you keep in mind that no flat statement about trout fishing is ever completely true. What I started to say was: Many small-stream trout, though cautious, are also a bit grabby in their feeding habits, even to the point of not being too selective about fly pattern. They may well spook at your first wrong move, but they also have the charming habit of eating a fly that is less than an exact anatomical copy of the naturals on the water.

I've always liked them for that.

They are also known to "gorge themselves greedily" and "lose all caution"—to quote a pair of fishing cliches—when something like a heavy caddis hatch or a windfall of grasshoppers comes along. Maybe in that sense small-stream trout really are the stuff of fly-fishing legend. You read about feeding frenzies on the big rivers, and maybe you stand around on windy August days with a Henry's Fork Hopper tied to your leader waiting for them, but so often the trout just seem to know better than to get silly.

A Separate Discipline

Fly fishing for trout in small streams is no harder, or easier, than fishing for them in rivers and lakes, but I think it's noticeably different, maybe even to the point of being a separate discipline within the sport. In many cases, the basic mechanics of it (show fly to fish, fish eats fly, etc.) are pretty simple, but getting to that point can be what many fisherpeople commonly refer to as "a real bitch."

The small stream is a tightly woven, finely balanced, diminutive environment, and it's not all that easy for a big clumsy fly fisherman to insinuate himself into it unnoticed. And, as we all know, once you *are* noticed, the jig is up.

So, for starters, we're talking about a high degree of stealth: the ability to slide into the situation without disturbing it, to avoid looming over the water like a diving osprey, to keep the shadows of human and fly rod off the water, to not bounce the sometimes soft banks of a meadow stream, or splash around loudly in the water. To be there, but also not there, in the finest tradition of the hunter.

That can be tough because we human beings have gotten it into our heads that we're somehow in charge of things on this planet—probably because we're the ones who can do the most damage—and so we stomp around as if we own the place, which we probably don't. Go stomping around on a small trout stream like you own it and see what happens.

Addressing a small trout stream properly is usually a matter of relaxing and slowing the pace, of realizing that there is no receptionist, no names on the office doors (no doors at all, in fact), and you don't have an appointment. You become sort of catlike, and with that in mind it's only a bit of thought and caution that gets you within casting range of a particular trout, or at least of the spot where that theoretical trout ought to be.

Casting

Stalking small streams can take a little bit of physical prowess, but mostly it's a matter of attitude and understanding. But casting, well, that can take real skill. The modern fly-fishing industry is largely geared to distance, and so are modern fly fishers. The "best" fly caster you know is the guy who can cast the farthest, right? I grant you it's not easy, and I'm always impressed by those rare people who can lay out the whole line and a couple of feet of backing. But on many small streams it's more likely the problem will be to deliver your leader and maybe a few yards of line with great accuracy, while on your knees behind a bush with a stand of sixty-foot-tall trees behind you, without spooking the trout with the motion of your rod. This is an entirely different business, but doing it well takes every bit as much skill.

Okay, maybe that's an extreme example. You can find spots like that on most creeks, but, except for the smallest and brushiest of them, you can just move on upstream to an easier place. But you probably won't. You're a fly fisherman, after all, and you know the most difficult spots sometimes hide the biggest trout.

Fly fishing small streams can be problematic at times, and it's probably fair to say that if you don't lose a few flies and tangle your leader in a few bushes you're not really trying. Still, I think the small stream is one fishing situation where the fly rod is unarguably the best, most effective method. The water isn't too deep, the casts aren't too long, and the food organisms are fairly small, by which I mean trout-fly-sized bugs rather than jointed-Rapala-sized baitfish. It's the kind of thing that gave birth to the sport in the first place: insect imitations fished at short ranges.

Sure, in recent decades fly fishing has evolved to cover longer casts with Shooting Head lines, deeper water with Sink-Tips, and streamers too big for most fly boxes. Apparently the idea is to be able to manage anything a spin fisherman can do, which is just fine. Naturally, there are discussions going on about whether or not some of the more extreme methods are really "fly fishing" in some pure, rarified, but still undefined sense. That seems to be very important to a lot of fly fishers and it's an interesting question, although I don't consider it crucial to my very existence. When a questionable technique comes along, my first impulse isn't to ask, "Is it fly fishing?" but, "Is it legal?"

I don't want to get into that too deeply except to say that small-stream fishing probably *is* pure fly fishing, if only because just about everything you'll ever find yourself doing on a little trout creek will be pretty traditional.

Now it's true that some small streams are pounded hard by fishermen but, as trout waters go, it's the creeks that are most likely to wander off by themselves away from roads and parking lots. Even in areas where a good deal of fly fishing goes on, there are usually some little streams out there somewhere that are more or less unspoiled.

I don't know about you, but I can get tired of fishing in a crowd, even when the fishing itself is real good. I do it, of course. I mean, who could pass up those famous rivers where the trout are big and smart and where the regular hatches are laid out for you on the back cover of the local fly shop's catalog? I can even be sociable and have made some friends along trout rivers, but to me a large part of fly fishing is the quiet and the solitude.

I enjoy listening to the sounds of the woods (or fields or marshes or whatever) that are undisturbed except by me and whoever I happen to be with. I enjoy being able to rest a good pool for as long as I can stand to without worrying about the next guy not understanding what I'm doing and fishing through, and I'm downright stuck on the idea that the creek stretching out in front of me is fresh: that I'll be the first one to fish it today, or maybe this week, or maybe even . . . well, let's not lose our grip on reality here.

I like the critters, too. On heavily fished rivers either the animals have all been chased away or they're so tame they stand there looking at you with all the wildness of dairy cows. On little seldom-traveled creeks the deer, grouse, squirrels, and such may be innocently cocksure or honestly bewildered at seeing you, but either way they're more likely to act like real animals.

For that matter, the trout can be like that, too. They probably haven't seen nearly as many fishermen as the trout down the valley in the big, famous river, and they may not be covered by the same catch-and-release or slot-limit regulations, either, although in some cases they are and in others they should be.

These fish are more likely to spook right off the bat because they haven't yet learned—like their counter-parts down in the catch-and-release area—that it's the flies, not the legs and shadows of fishermen, that they have to be careful of. By the same token, they haven't had their natural, hungry, aggressive curios-ity trained out of them, so they often won't stop to count the segments on your Blue Quill or measure it against a natural before eating it.

In a way they're easier to catch and in a way they're harder but, all in all, I think they act more like trout were meant to. And that can be refreshing.

Not that I have anything against catch-and-release regulations. If nothing else, they're the reason why there are any trout left in many of the best rivers around the country. I don't even think it's a drawback that they can sometimes make the fishing incredibly difficult, because that's fun, too.

Hell, *all* fishing is fun.

If there's a down side to small streams, it would have to be the size of the trout in some of them. How big a trout gets (discounting fishing pressure for the moment) depends largely on how long he lives and how well he eats, and that, in turn, depends on the quality of his habitat. There are small creeks in many parts of the country that are deep, rich, bug-infested, and filled with nice big trout. Many of them are well known by now, but a few have escaped the mobs by virtue of being either very remote or private.

I guess I have a populist streak in me because private trout streams tend to rub me the wrong way, although my feathers can be smoothed some by an invitation to fish there. And remote streams, when they pan out, are always worth the hike in.

In any case, the best small streams are every bit as good as, and sometimes better than, the best big rivers.

Many other little creeks are less than cosmic in terms of big trout, but I think any stream with, let's say, nine- to twelve-inch trout of any species in it is well worth fishing. If said creek is pretty (as most are), if it's fairly quiet and out of the way, if the fish are healthy and wild, if you're alone or in very sparse company, well, look at all the charm you've piled on.

And while we're at it, let's not give up on those big fish just yet. Take little No-name Creek. You know, the tributary to the tributary to the big river where everyone fishes. It flows year-round and is known to have at least a few small trout in it, but it doesn't look like much where it goes under the road, and the only real fishing pressure comes from a couple of local kids with cane poles and cans of worms.

But it *does* flow out of the National Forest and there's a lot of country up in there, not all of which is like it is down here. Maybe there's a stretch of beaver ponds up there somewhere, and/or a half dozen bend

A fourteen-inch rainbow is a good small-stream trout.

pools across a little meadow, and/or a headwater lake or two. And all that (maybe) on a little stream that few people fish because it doesn't look all that great where they can see it from the road, and because they probably never heard of it before. (Believe it or not, some fishermen only fish streams about which books have been written.)

That's the kind of thing that can get you to thinking. Even medium-sized trout are plenty of fun to catch, and if there's some better water up there (it doesn't take much) there could be some big fish.

To my way of thinking, small-stream "big" starts at about twelve inches and goes up from there. Around home it seldom goes past fifteen inches, and then not too often, but that's okay. A healthy fifteen-inch-long trout is a nice fish anywhere, and on a small stream it's a hog.

I guess it's the size of the trout (or, I should say, the *suspected* size of the trout) that keeps many serious fly fishermen off the small streams. To be perfectly honest, if the deal being proposed was that you get the best of all the good things fly fishing offers in return for catching smaller trout, I'd take it. Actually, I did make that very deal with myself once and was perfectly happy with it. Then I caught my first sixteen-inch trout from a small stream, after which I was even happier.

But, also to be honest, if you get into small streams you will catch your share of what you consider to be little trout. So let me introduce an idea—just something to kick around: Maybe your stature as a fly fisherman isn't determined by how big a trout you can catch, but by how *small* a trout you can catch without being disappointed, and, of course, without losing the faith that there's a bigger one in there.

Sneaking Around on Your Hands and Knees

I think stealth, and its various manifestations, rates its own chapter. It's an underrated skill in fly fishing that's often listed after casting, entomology, wading, and even fly tying in order of importance, but I could introduce you to several fly fishers around here who can't cast worth a damn, don't know a mayfly from a barn owl, and wade like buffaloes, but who still catch lots of trout because they know how to sneak up on them.

These guys do most of their fishing in the little mountain creeks and they mostly don't look like—or consider themselves to be—among the upscale, gentleman fly-fishing types, but they are very, very good. You can learn a lot from people like this, not the least being that you don't need five hundred dollars' worth of rod and reel and a designer vest to catch some fish. When I *do* show up with an expensive fly rod, they usually don't give me too much grief about it. I've lived here for eleven years and by now most of the boys figure I'm okay, even if I'm still a little stuck-up in the tackle department.

How Trout See

There's been a lot of work done on how trout see, especially how they see things on the surface of the water and out on the bank. I don't understand some of it, but I understand what fly fishers have always known:

namely, that the fish can see you, and when they do, they don't like it.

Even if young trout don't have a genetic predisposition to being afraid of things looming above them, they sure learn it when they see their brothers and sisters get eaten by herons, kingfishers, and such. *Most* of their brothers and sisters, in fact. The survival rate for baby trout is thin.

I'm sure trout don't understand what a fisherman is and what kind of danger they're in from one—even though they seem like they do at times—but they know you're out there where all the bad things come from and they are definitely on to you.

You'd think the really big trout who have less to fear would get over that, but they don't, of course. They actually get worse—or better, depending on your point of view. They're the first to spook and they stay spooked the longest. It's a case of what my friend Koke Winter calls, "not forgetting how you got where you are."

So, step one is to keep the trout from seeing you. On bigger water this is often done with the long cast, long drift, and/or long, fine leader while the fisherman is standing at least thirty feet away concentrating on throwing a downstream hook cast into an upstream wind, an exercise that's partly athletic and partly intellectual. At its best, this is graceful and dignified. At its worst, you're at least standing upright.

In many small-stream situations, that just doesn't work. If you're thirty feet above or below the trout in question, you could be around the next bend and out of sight. If you're that far off to the side, you're back in the trees trying to thread a tight-looped cast between the trunks behind and in front of you. I've actually seen that done, by the way, but only by the very best casters and then usually just to show off. Given the scale of most small streams, you just can't get that far away and still fish, or even still see the water in some spots.

Usually, getting close means staying low. As I said, I don't fully understand the dynamics of the trout's window of vision, but I know that the higher you are, and the more prominent your silhouette is, the more likely they are to see you. And, because a trout's eyes are set on the sides of its head, like a deer's or a rabbit's, it can see things in a wider range than we binocular-vision types. Trout are also keyed, again like deer and rabbits, to see more movement than shape.

I think the first step in approaching a small stream isn't a step at all. My friend A. K. Best says you can spot a good fly fisherman from a great distance: he's the guy who stops way back from the water and looks things over. He doesn't already have a fly tied to his tippet because he doesn't know which one he's going to use yet. If he's wearing a pack, he takes it off to stretch his shoulders. He may sit cross-legged on the ground or get comfortable on a convenient stump. A fisherman of great inner peace may take the opportunity to build a new hand-tied leader from the butt section out, watching the stream carefully between knots.

Maybe that's an even greater skill than stealth—the ability to not be in such a big hurry all the time. A trout stream will often give you all the information you need to fish it properly, but the parade of clues moves at its own pace, and a good look at the water takes time.

Like most, A. K. and I look for rises first. Rises are often the only sign of trout you'll see from any distance, and they also mean you'll stand a good chance of being able to fish dry flies. They will also tell you where at least some of the trout are, and, by extrapolation, where some others might be along the rest of the stream, at least for a while.

Sneaking Up

There was a time when I would simply start sneaking up on the first rising trout I spotted, which seemed logical. I mean, those are the fish you're going to cast to, and you have to sneak, so you put your sneak *on them*, right?

Well, yes and no. The thing is, not every trout in the stream is rising to mayflies out in that tongue of current. Some are in other places, too, like maybe right in the spot you step in on your way to the proper casting position. Those fish spook wildly, and in the seconds it takes you to realize you should have considered this somewhat differently, they charge through those rising trout, who figure something is up and spook themselves.

Dirt and pine needles still cling to the knees of your hip boots from your approach to the stream—that beautiful stalk that had you on hands and knees at least once—but now there you stand. Without making so much as a single cast, you've blundered in and screwed it up and, although this may not be nearly as important as other things you've screwed up in the past, it still gives you that familiar feeling of loss and hopelessness: a feeling that should be avoided when at all possible.

Luckily, it doesn't always happen like that, but it happens often. When you're in one of those moods where you really want to catch some fish, you should probably assume it *will* happen.

For a long time, I always made better—that is, more successful—stalks on creeks when there were no trout rising. That's because, in that situation, I couldn't fool myself with limited information. With no fish showing, I figured they could be just about anywhere and proceeded on that assumption. I guess I had to be pounded on the head by the connection for a long time, but now I try to always proceed on that assumption. At times it's been rewarding: times when the rising trout you could see from so far away were actually a bunch of little ones, while the few big fish were hugging the near bank where before I'd have just waded in.

Those times when the extra care of the slow, cautious approach wouldn't have made any difference didn't even seem like wasted effort. They seemed like good practice. A. K. says you can also sometimes tell the *bad* fly fisherman from a distance: he's the guy who's standing in the water he should be casting to.

I have picked up, over the years, a kind of shuffling, knees flexed, back bent, creeping walk that I fall into when approaching a spooky-looking piece of water. I copied it from other fishermen I saw doing it because it looked neat and felt satisfying, but it actually seems to help some. I'm six feet tall, but when I crouch down like that I'm more like four and a half. Yes, I did measure it. The top of my head is no higher than the thermostat on the living room wall, and on days when my bum knee bends pretty well, I can get even shorter.

I find this a good place to start. Sometimes it lets me get close enough to make the cast, though in the stickier spots it just lets me get close enough to see where I really have to be. More than that, it puts me in the appropriate mood. To sneak properly you have to adjust your sense of dignity, and once you start creeping around the woods like a gnome, you are more or less with the program.

Some people have more trouble getting into this than

Author using bankside brush for cover. Photo by Dan Dzubay.

others, though it was never much of a stretch for me. I think it helps if you have a basically duplicitous nature and played a lot of pranks as a kid.

Speed, or lack thereof, is another important element of stalking. If you hustle along at the normal human pace (you know, the one that says, in plain body language, "Let's make some time, dammit, we don't have all day") you'll spook trout, not to mention deer, chipmunks, nuthatches, and etc. Everything in the woods will run from you because it's clear you don't belong there, have no idea what you're doing, and are probably up to no good. On the other hand, you can develop a real advantage over trout and other wild animals once you come to realize that you do, in fact, have all day.

In other words, move slowly.

In some situations you can also take advantage of available cover. I like small streams with tree-lined banks not only because they're pretty, but because you can hide behind the trees and get a lot closer to the fish. Even if you're not crouching behind the trunk of a big willow, you are just another upright shape among many to the trout, and if you walk very slowly you may well go unnoticed.

Staying in the trees means you'll also be in the shade and against a dark backdrop. I think both of those things help to hide you. It's been my experience that you'll spook trout more easily if you're out in the direct sun and silhouetted against the sky. I think they simply pick you out, thinking the fish equivalent of, "That wasn't there before," or maybe, "That's not a tree, it's wearing a hat." Staying in the available shadows will often let you get closer and will also serve to cover your movements.

Speaking of shadows, you throw one yourself, and so

Using jumbled boulders in a stretch of pocket water for cover.

does your fly rod. Either one is guaranteed to scare the hell out of the fish. Try to maintain a sense of where shadows, especially yours, are falling.

I've met a few fly fishers who wear camouflage for small-stream fishing and some others who say you *should* wear it, even though they don't. I guess that strikes me as a little extreme—or maybe just a little too serious—but it certainly couldn't hurt and might even help for all I know.

Personally, I'm of the school of thought that stops short of full camo fatigues, but says you should dress in drab, dark colors. I guess I don't get all that concerned about this, but I do leave the white straw cowboy hats and blaze-orange hunting shirts at home when I'm going out to fish a small stream.

I'll take that back. I wear a bright orange shirt when I'm out fishing in deer or elk season on the premise that it's better to spook a few trout than to get shot. I actually have faith that most hunters won't whang away at something they can't see clearly, but it's not a bad idea for them just to know you're around. When you think about it, a drably dressed fly fisher creeping quietly along a trout stream in the woods can look pretty suggestive to someone who wants to see legal game.

The fly fishing is good in the fall and I'm usually out quite a bit in the big-game seasons, wearing at least an orange shirt, if not the baseball cap that goes with it. In fact, it's quite a few years of more or less successfully sneaking up on trout dressed like that that's convinced me the color of your clothes isn't what's important. Good hunters dressed in orange sneak up on deer all the time, and deer are smarter than trout.

However you're dressed, try keeping your rod tip low.

A skinny fly rod isn't as scary to trout as is the looming shape of a person, but it's movement, and in their limited imaginations the fish seem to glimpse a diving kingfisher or the long sharp beak of a heron and they'll hit the dirt before waiting for their suspicions to be confirmed. It's a proven survival tactic and therefore automatic. The best small-stream fishermen I've watched work—the ones I've tried to copy—point their rods behind them, aimed parallel to the ground, when they have to stalk. Once in place, they'll often use a sidearm cast to deliver the fly.

The Sidearm Cast

A. K. and I fish together a lot and I have many photos of him. He's a great subject for the camera because he looks and dresses the part of the archetypal fly fisherman—right down to floppy hat and pipe—is a fine caster, and has this tendency to catch fish, which is great for the action shots. If he ever decides to give up his fly-tying business, he could probably make a living renting himself to outdoor writers as a professional model.

Anyway, one of my favorite shots is of A. K. casting to a tiny little creek just outside of the Indian Peaks Wilderness area in Colorado. On the left of the frame is the stream. It's a stretch of fast pocket water no more than a few yards wide that flows out of sight into some tall stately fir trees. In the foreground is yet another fir, and peeking around that, dressed in a rain slicker that is, not entirely coincidentally, exactly the same green as the fir needles, is A. K.

He's fishing a short upstream sidearm cast that keeps his rod tip behind the view of the upstream-facing trout and places only the fly and a foot or so of leader on the water.

This is not quite a "find the fly fisherman in this picture" kind of shot, but it's close, and I've used it in slide shows to illustrate how to get close to trout in shallow water.

Each situation is unique. My friend Gil Lipp and I were once fishing a little creek within sight of the head-water lake it flowed out of. We had scrambled up a slope to bypass a steep chute in which no trout could have lived, and we came upon a wide, slow, shallow pool that was full of rising cutthroats.

The day was bright and calm, the pool was shallow and clear, set out in open marginal tundra with only a few stunted two-foot-tall spruce trees near it for cover. The trout were nice ones: the smallest maybe a foot long, the largest more like fourteen or fifteen inches. We crouched fifty yards away and twenty feet above the pool and I offered it to Gil.

I don't know why, exactly. Maybe I didn't think I could handle it and didn't want to blow it in front of a perceptive, critical audience. Or maybe I wanted to be the audience myself. This was a number of years ago, but I think it was after I'd come to realize that watching a good caster work a tricky spot is almost as much fun as trying it yourself—and it's educational, too.

Gil duck-walked down the slope (on good, strong, rock-climber's knees) and then went on all fours—all threes, actually, with one hand holding the seven-foot rod out behind him—until he could kneel behind one of those squat, Oriental-looking trees.

It was at this point that I became sorry for being so generous. The tactic was pretty obvious and, except for the duck-walk, I could have handled it very nicely myself.

We never talked about how he picked his fish, but it seems to have gone something like this: He knew this was a one-fish spot and that a cast that lined any of those trout would spook them all and turn it instantaneously into a no-fish spot, so he chose the largest trout that was closest to him. This is perfectly logical, of course, but you still have to overcome your natural sense of greed to see it clearly, especially since the very largest fish you can see is always in the wrong spot.

Gil hooked the fish on the second or third cast with, if I remember correctly, a #16 Adams dry fly. He stayed on his knees while playing it, but that was just a gesture because, with the trout's first wiggle, every other fish in the pool stopped rising and vanished. All in all, it was a sweet job of fly fishing.

I've been back to that pool a few times since then and have even caught a few fish from it, though never more than one per stalk. The very next time, later that same summer and with a different fishing partner, I generously offered the pool just above it to the other guy, knowing that it would then be my turn when we got to the one I really wanted. This is known as "home courtsmanship" and I think it's fair as long as you don't abuse it.

Granted, these are extreme cases dredged up to make a point and not the kind of thing you'll find on every small stream. On most of my own small-stream expeditions I do not spend the whole day sneaking around on my hands and knees and probably wouldn't enjoy it too much if I did. Still, I like it when it's appropriate and I think it actually gets me into more and larger trout on something like a regular basis. In some spots it is simply the only way to fish if you want to catch anything.

I've even had some quite good fly fishers tell me there are no trout "worth catching" in some of the creeks I like. In some cases that's nothing more than big-fish chauvinism whereby one's manhood is somehow gauged by how big a fish it takes to get him excited, but in others it's evidence that they just don't know how to fish small waters. You can't splash around in a small stream like you would on a half-mile-wide river and expect to catch anything but the smallest, most innocent trout.

To Wade or Not to Wade

Speaking of splashing around, try not to. Now, I love wading. It can be a lot of fun in both the pastoral and the thrills-and-chills departments, and the whole idea of being in the water with the fish is one of the things that gives fly fishing its feelings of immediacy and deep involvement. It's also a great way to mess things up for yourself when you're trying to fish at short ranges.

My basic rule for small streams is: Stay out of the water if at all possible. I don't find this easy because I really want to get in there with the fish and look for excuses to do it: the trees are too close for a steeple cast, the wind is blowing the wrong way, the sun is in my eyes, and so on. You know.

The fact is, casting is invariably easier when you're standing in the stream because you have that open lane behind you for the back cast, but it doesn't make much difference how easy the casting is if you've spooked all the fish.

I once tried to fool myself on this account by going

fishing in hiking boots instead of waders, but that was unsatisfactory. Your feet are just going to get wet if you're fooling around a stream, even if you don't actually get into it, and in the normal course of things you'll want to cross it from time to time. All I succeeded in doing was wrecking a decent pair of boots.

Once again, I'm talking about extreme cases. On many small streams you'll do plenty of wading and it will work out just fine, especially if you go about it slowly and carefully, doing your best to keep the noise down and not cause too many ripples on the water.

I think you can cut yourself a little slack in faster water where the trout's visibility is lower, and maybe also on windy days when the ripples you make won't be noticed on the already ruffled surface.

By the same token, tremendous care has to be taken when wading something like slow-flowing, glassy, shallow water on a bright, calm day. It's possible to do—and a real occasion for self-congratulation when you can pull it off—but it takes the kind of slow determination you see in a vegetable.

Even if you can manage to stay out of the water altogether, there will be times when you have to consider your footfalls on the bank. This is especially important around beaver ponds and in other marshy, peat-boggy sorts of places where the ground feels like an old mattress. Spongy ground can telegraph a footstep for many yards.

Trout hear vibrations through their sensitive lateral lines. That was hard for me to relate to until a fisheries biologist suggested I think of trout as having little ears from head to tail down both sides of their bodies.

Resting a Pool
Another practical part of stealth is the ability to rest

a pool. Maybe there's a big fish in there, the biggest one you've seen all day, and you spooked him with a bad cast. You can always leave and try to find another one, but sometimes there *isn't* another one, or if there is, someone else is fishing for him. Or maybe you made your best stalk, but all the fish stopped rising anyway.

Either way, if you haven't disturbed things too badly, you can usually rest the place until the fish come back. It can take ten minutes, an hour, or until the same time the following day and is a real test of your fortitude, but it's also downright satisfying. When the trout finally start rising, there you are, undetected. "Boy," you say to yourself, "am I crafty or what?"

Naturally, how long you rest a pool will be based on a personal formula that takes into account the size of the fish in question and your current state of mind, as well as lesser factors like the alignment of the planets and how long ago lunch was. There are days when it doesn't work and, of course, you can give up at any time, but understand this: Once you've committed yourself to waiting a spot out, to give up is to accept defeat— Stream 1, Fisherman 0. It's one of the unwritten rules of the sport. If you stick it out until it gets dark, you can call it a draw.

The joys of pool-resting are an acquired taste and for years I couldn't manage it for more than a few minutes. Now I take it as a challenge, a test of my inner composure. It's as close as I can come to honest meditation and I believe I've actually discovered some things about the hidden workings of reality while sitting in the grass, resting pools. I'd tell you what those things are, but I forgot them all when the trout started to rise again.

It's actually a good idea to rest a pool for at least a few minutes before you make the first cast to it because your new, closer perspective may let you spot fish you hadn't seen before. Maybe nice big fish that, if you were in too much of a hurry, you would never have known were there.

Remember that a trout, however bright and colorful he is once in your hand, is well camouflaged when seen against the bottom. Remember also that you won't always see "a fish." Look for flashes of color, movements, shadows, streamlined shapes, the whites of mouths opening and closing, the crisp wavings of tails.

A pair of polarized sunglasses will be a big help, but they're not as important as the ability to just sit there quietly for a little while, looking at, and into, the water.

One more thing about pool-resting: Do it sooner rather than later. Once you've spooked the trout, a few dozen more casts will do no good and more than a little harm.

At its best, fishing of any kind requires an almost fierce patience, but fly fishing is deceptive because you're always doing something (usually casting) so it doesn't seem like you have to be patient at all.

But you do.

One thought that helps me with all this is that it's the trout in question that matters (or the pool or the run you want to fish) and not total numbers of trout caught. I think I have the most fun fly fishing small streams when I can get into that nice, contemplative state of mind where the difficulty of the approach, accuracy of the cast, trickiness of the drift, and so on are all an integral part of the single fish caught well.

Most fishermen believe that, but it seems like small-stream nuts have a special handle on it. For instance, I once received a compliment on my casting. (I feel free to bring it up because it was one of so few.) A man who'd been watching me fish a little creek near here said, "You really know how to use that thing, don't ya?"

"Yeah, well," I said, not used to getting compliments, "but I'm not catching any fish."

"So what?" the guy said.

And then A. K. called just the other day to tell me about a particularly difficult fish he'd just caught. He told me all about the stalk and the cast and the many drifts with different flies and finally the strike. And then he hung up without bothering to mention how big the trout had been or if he'd caught any others that day. In fact, he didn't even say that he actually caught that fish, just that he'd finally gotten it to take the fly.

Of course, these are the same people who will spend more money than they can spare and risk drowning, freezing, and all kinds of other hazards in order to catch huge trout, but that only seems paradoxical if you expect any of this to make sense.

Courtesy

If you buy the importance of stealth in small-stream fishing, you also have to buy the importance of courtesy to other fishermen. What you know about not trashing the water for yourself should also be practiced in behalf of the other guy on general principles.

Now, A. K. and I have been known to fish very close together on small streams—"in each other's hip pockets" as someone once said—but remember that we are old and solid fishing partners who know each other so well that we can carry on an entire conversation with grunts and hand signals. We can fish the same small pool, alternating our casts so we don't snag each other's lines, and end up spending the afternoon exchanging recipes for venison burgers between fish. But that's the kind of thing that should only be done with friends you're so close to that common courtesy has become obsolete. All others deserve as much space as you can give them.

When you meet someone on the creek, try to remember how small the stream is and how easy it is to spook every fish in it. Go farther around him than you would on a river. Stay well away from the water he's fishing and be careful of your shadow. Ideally, what you should leave your colleague here is a stretch of totally undisturbed stream. The surest way to do that is to reel in, get out of the water, get as close to out of sight of the stream as is realistic and *then* pass. I know, it's not always possible. If you come on another fisherman in a narrow steep-sided box canyon, one or the other of you has a problem, but how many times does that happen? Usually it's not impossible to be courteous, it's just difficult.

At the risk of sounding preachy, just do it: climb the steep bank, wade through the thick brush, thread your rod through the trees, and be nice. In those rare situations where this would involve a 200-foot unprotected ascent of an overhanging sandstone cliff, at least stop and have a conference with the guy. Maybe you can work something out. Do not just blast through figuring he'll understand. He won't. Would you?

Some of my friends and I have had a lot of practice at this because the only way for two fishermen to work the same small stream in the same direction is to leapfrog each other. We pass each other many times in a day's fishing, and if I spook the last hole by being too clumsy or in too much of a rush, none of the people I fish with regularly are too polite to mention it to me, usually in terms just short of assault.

The one thing I've learned from this is that if you take the extra trouble, the other guy will do the same for you. And the extra trouble usually isn't that much of a stretch. If you've already climbed the bank anyway, step back into the trees and disappear altogether.

I think it's also best to cut your colleague some decent slack in whatever direction he's fishing. That is, you'll naturally get back in far enough from him that you won't spook the spot he's fishing, but why not consider leaving him the next few holes, too? I guess I have an advantage over some because many of the creeks I fish regularly are not all that heavily fished. If you meet three or four other people in a day, it's crowded. So I've gotten into the habit of going at least out of sight of whoever I pass. Part of that is just being a nice guy (if I do say so myself), but I find there's a practical advantage to not having someone around who could see you fall in or hang your fly in a tree. That's because if there's someone there to see it, you'll do it. Of course, if you catch a big fish, there won't be anyone around to see that, either, but you can't have it both ways.

If I come upon someone sitting on the bank or just standing there with his rod under his arm, I assume he's resting the water, communing with nature, or a little of both. Whatever, the spot he's in is *his spot* and I go around, although I'll usually at least say hello. The only time I don't speak to other fishermen is when there are too many of them.

A Crisp, Low,
Sidearm Roll Cast

What I'm going to do here is invent a small stream that has on it all the different kinds of water I want to talk about. Mostly it'll be the little St. Vrain "River" over here because it has so many different kinds of habitat, but I'll also be grafting on stretches of other streams (all real ones) in the interests of completeness. Think of it as poetic license. Fishing writers do this kind of thing all the time.

I was going to give it a name, but I can't think of anything that wouldn't be too cute. If you're thinking back to No-name Creek, which I mentioned earlier, let me just say that there really *is* a No-name Creek.

Your first glimpse of a small stream may be way down on its drainage where it empties into the river you're fishing. If it's high summer and the weather is hot, you should probably even seek this place out because the cooler creek flowing into the warmer river will often attract trout.

You might also want to look for that same spot in the spring when the river is off-color from the runoff. With any luck, there will be a stretch along the bank where a plume of clear water lies up against the turbid water of the river. Trout have been known to collect at spots like that, and right along that dividing line is a good place to fish nymphs.

How the creek looks where it enters the river naturally depends on the shape of the surrounding countryside. Let's say this one is in fairly flat, wooded terrain. It's probably wide here, by small-stream standards, but the trees keep it nicely shaded, except maybe for an hour either side of noon. It's made mostly of slow-moving pools and glides, and as you look up it, the only current marks you see are where the water steps over and around a few rocks between one flat and the next.

This far down, it's probably about as large as the typical small stream gets, which means you may have to search a little for a spot where you can cross without shipping water over the tops of your hip boots. On the other hand, there are few casting positions—including right in the middle of the stream—where you don't have to glance over your shoulder to make sure your backcast isn't going into a tree.

As pretty and fishy-looking as it is here, you can bet it's been a regular stop for passing fly fishers, so there's probably a fisherman's trail leading up one side of it or the other. Don't follow it. Fisherman's trails almost always go too close to the water. I think they're made by crafty locals so tourist fly fishermen will walk along them, spook the trout, figure the place is fished out, and go home.

I always want to see rising trout in water like this, and I often do. If there are any insects on the water at all, even just a few scattered ants and beetles, at least a few fish will be working at the top. You can see them clearly in the almost glassy current. As a rule, trout seem to rise freely in small streams, probably because it's so easy for them.

It's a beautiful sight—trout rising casually in slow glide—but I try not to let it shake my composure. I remind myself that it's often the younger, smaller trout who are the most eager about coming to the surface in open water for the odd bug.

If a big fish is rising in a situation like this, it seems like nine times out of ten he's in a much more sheltered spot: maybe along an undercut bank or beneath some overhanging branches or in the slick water behind a rock. All things being equal, the largest trout will be in the best feeding spots, best in terms of numbers of insects, availability of cover, slower currents, or all three. In a slow, open stretch of water like this, that good spot is often along a bank.

Often. It's a word you have to use in every other sentence when writing about trout and trout fishing because even though there are rules firm enough to base safe assumptions on, there are also plenty of notable exceptions. For instance. Sometimes one of those fish rising out in the open water will, in fact, be a nice big one. Maybe there are more bugs on the water than you think and he's been lured out to feed. There could be something that's not evident about the current and the bottom structure right there that makes it a better spot than it looks like. Or maybe he's just a big, sassy trout with a taste for ants.

Spotting Fish

I always like to watch the riseforms for a while to see if I can determine how big the fish are. You can't always tell, especially if they're rising lazily and not moving much water, but there are sometimes subtle hints, like the bubble left behind by a dimpling rise. A big fish makes a big bubble.

If you can see the fish, you'll know, and I will sometimes creep around a bit, not to get into a casting position, but just to try and see the fish. This kind of thing can get you crawling around on your stomach if you're not careful.

My friend Gil has been known to carry a small pair of binoculars for spotting fish and, although I've used them myself only a few times, I think it's a great idea. It's also a good way to spot those bank risers in the shade on the far side of the stream that can be damned hard to see at times. Still, like so many good ideas, I haven't taken it up myself, maybe because I try to keep things fairly simple and even at that end up lugging around enough stuff as it is. And anyway, if I got into using binoculars on a regular basis, I'd have to invent detachable polarizing filters for them because I can't look through binocs and sunglasses at the same time.

Casting Upstream and Down

So, you've finally picked out a fish that looks like a good one and you've managed to do it without spooking him. For the sake of argument, let's say you've also determined what he's rising to and have a fly something like it in your box (two rash assumptions, I know).

Some will use an upstream and others a downstream cast in a situation like this, and if done right either will work. I see two basic advantages to the upstream dry-fly cast. One is that the fish will be facing into the current, so when you cast from below him he's facing away from you. You're on his blind side and can get closer to him, either by wading or staying on the bank. The other is that when he takes the fly (okay, *if* he takes the fly) you'll be setting back into his mouth and will be more likely to get a good solid hook-up.

With the *downstream* drift, which I usually prefer, you are in front of the fish, but that's okay because you can almost always get a much longer float casting down-stream than up, so you can be farther away. It's also just plain easier to get a long drag-free float from up-stream.

With the downstream float you can also drop your line on the water well above the trout's cone of vision, while on the upstream cast, the line, and certainly the leader, land much closer to him. The upstream caster needs a much longer leader to keep the line away from the fish than the downstream caster does, and the longer the leader is, the harder it is to cast accurately. In fact, the whole business of tremendously long dry-fly leaders, and all the difficulties that come with them, came largely from the traditional style of upstream casting.

It's also said that with a downstream drift the fish sees the fly first rather than the leader, which he sees first on an upstream delivery. I don't know if that makes a difference or not, but enough good fishing writers say it does—sometimes even backing it up with under-water photography—that I'll say it again here. It does sound reasonable, although it fails to explain all the difficult fish that have been caught on upstream casts.

The one real disadvantage to the downstream drift is in the area of hooking. When you set your hook on the strike, you're pulling it toward the front of the trout's mouth instead of back into the corner of his jaw. That means you'll hook more fish in the lip and will probably miss more altogether.

And then there's the matter of line mending. The up-stream caster usually has to mend his line in the air to get the right hook or slack in the leader to counteract the current and keep the fly from dragging. He also has to judge beforehand what the current will do to his drift. Trial and error in this department is a good way to put the fish down before you get it figured out.

With a downstream drift, mending the line properly is sometimes as easy as simply picking it up and putting it where you want it, using the rod tip as a pointer. That's naturally assuming you're far enough from the trout in question that all the commotion won't bother him.

In the end, I guess it's as much a matter of style as anything else. From my own experience I'd say the guy who consistently casts upstream to rising trout has to be a better caster than the one who drifts the fly down to him. That's why I prefer the latter method, although I try to be at least a fair hand at both because, for one reason or another, you don't always have the choice.

For that matter, this whole discussion of how to approach rising trout in smooth current is a matter of style, and the downstream cast is not even the style I use all the time. In my best vision of the sport, I see myself spotting the fish I want, stalking him carefully, and hooking him on the first—or at least the second—long, perfect downstream cast.

Fine, everyone needs a vision to guide him, and that's mine, but there are other moods and other ways.

One of them is to "fish the water." In this scenario you approach the same stretch of stream—the glide with a few fish rising here and there, including the big one along the bank—but this time you slide carefully into the water. You wade so slowly that the few ripples you cause are washed gently downstream and away from the fish. You cast upstream, fishing the tail of the glide where fish often lie, then the left bank, then the right, using all kinds of slack, snake, curve, and hook casts to get good dead drifts on the fly. You pay special attention to the rising trout, but you also cast to most of the other water in something like a fan pattern and are rewarded with a few surprise strikes. When you finish with the first glide, you wade slowly to the next while keeping your fly dry by false-casting it on a short line.

Hours later it's getting dark and you're wondering whether to stay for the possible evening rise or try to make it back to the car while you can still find it.

That's not a half-bad vision, either. It's rhythmic, almost hypnotic, and busy in a slowly paced way, while the "stalk-and-perfect-cast" approach is more determined and predatory. How you approach the stream is a matter of how you feel that day and whether you're in the mood to catch "The Fish" or "some fish." There's a big difference between those two attitudes, even though the results can be about the same.

Dry Flies

I favor the dry fly in water like this because, as I said, trout in shallow streams are seldom shy about coming to the surface. That, I believe, is because the surface is never very far away, and also because you're probably looking at a creek that is not what you'd call lousy with insects, so the fish will be tempted to at least inspect any reasonable-looking floating bug.

Even if there are no fish rising, I'll still usually try a dry fly first, concentrating on shaded banks, undercuts, overhanging branches, and the heads and tails of the pools: the classic holding spots, in other words. To me, one of the finest things in fly fishing is to cast a dry fly to a spot where no fish is rising—but where one ought to be—and have him come out of nowhere to take it.

I have a real fondness for dry flies and I like small

Undercut bank with exposed roots: an ideal trout spot.

streams because drys work so well on them, but there are other things that work, too.

Nymphs

Nymphs can be very effective, but the standard short-line nymphing technique is often a little clumsy on small streams. Short-lining is where you put a nymph on the end of the tippet, split-shot or Twist-ons a foot or so above it, and drift the whole thing through the deep holes. You fish the nymph on a slack line to let it bounce along the bottom in a natural, helpless-looking way, following the drift with the rod tip, always watching for the bump or hesitation in the floating part of the line or leader that indicates a take.

This is great in deeper water where you can get close enough to the fish without spooking them. The people who are really good at it usually wade to within a rod's length or so of where the fish are lying in a deep run, cinch on half a dozen BB-sized split-shot, and drift the nymph through again and again.

It's deadly, as they say.

A lighter-weight version of this can work well on small streams, but on the kind of slow-flowing glides we're talking about here you have to go down to the real bantam class. For one thing, you don't need much weight to get a fly to the bottom of three or four feet of slow water. For another, it's often disastrous to try to get that close.

What I usually end up doing is using a kind of modified wet-fly style. I'll use a long leader with either a single small split-shot or maybe half a Twist-on a foot to eighteen inches above the fly. I'll end up actually *fishing* the fly almost straight across the current to the run in question, but I'll cast as far upstream as I can manage so the weight splashing on the water is out of the trout's view and so the fly has time to sink by the time it gets to where I want it to be. And I'll stay as far away as I can, which is where it gets clumsy.

The best and easiest way to get a dead drift is to fish the weighted nymph rig directly under the rod tip, and that's how you try to do it on big water. The shallower and slower the water is, the farther back you have to be, and the farther back you have to be, the more conflicting currents you have working against your leader and dragging your fly. There are people who are much better at this than I am, but even the best nymph fishers I know tend to gravitate to the deeper, faster slots and plunge pools, leaving the shallow, quiet glides alone.

If I'm on this slow stretch of stream in the evening—and if there doesn't happen to be a riotous hatch going on—I'll sometimes try a streamer with a swinging downstream-and-across cast. I'll run it past big bottom rocks, noodle it through the tails of pools, and, on the longest, quietest glides, I'll feed it downstream and slowly hand-twist it back up. But the best spot is usually along the deepest bank, preferably an undercut. This is where, in my imagination at least, the big trout whose taste has turned from bugs to fish is lurking. Sometimes it's actually true.

Streamers

Around here, streamer fishing seems to be considered a big-river tactic, but it's surprisingly effective on small streams, especially, as I said, in the evenings, and also in creeks that hold brown trout. If I had to characterize the fish, I'd say that browns are hot for streamers, rainbows and brookies can be convinced, and cutthroats are pretty suspicious. But don't take that as gospel because if trout are anything they're unpredictable. I've had browns spook wildly from streamers and cutthroats (who are not supposed to like streamers much at all) chase them halfway across the stream. Sometimes the old trout personality profiles work and sometimes they don't.

It seems to me that a streamer, especially on a small stream, isn't something you need to fish with great patience and concentration in a single spot. If the fish is there and he wants it, he'll hit it the first or second time you swim it past him. If not, he's either been scared to death by this big fly shooting past, or he's just not interested. You're trying to trigger an aggressive response and that's not something a trout will ponder over, as he sometimes will with a slowly drifting dry fly.

You can cover a good deal of water fishing a few swings here and there with a streamer and I'll sometimes tie one on for the trip back out as it's getting dark. I tend to do that casually, because I'd usually rather fish down than just walk down, but more than once it's accounted for the biggest fish of the day, which is always a nice way to wrap things up.

Meadows

Following the same creek upstream, you come to a meadow. I seem to want to picture this in late August or maybe early September when the grass and wild grains are knee high and dull gold. Here the stream goes into a series of wide S curves. It's still the same small stream and it's shallow and riffly where it straightens out, but the bend pools on the outside of each curve are deeper than any of the water down below in the slow glides.

The bend pool is one of the finest pieces of trout

Willow-lined banks at the head of a meadow.

habitat there is. There will be almost endless variations on the theme, but the archetypal one is roughly half-moon-shaped with a riffle or fast chute at the top, a deep, slow cut along the outside bank, and a tail that tapers up into the next riffle. In a meadow, the current will probably have eaten out the far bank to make a deep dark undercut.

Undercut banks *can* be deep, quite often much deeper than they look. I've helped with electroshocking fish surveys on some small streams—when the crew had all the biologists and graduate students they needed but were still short a grunt or two—and have reached up into undercuts with an electrode on the end of a four-foot pole without touching the back end. Sure, they weren't all like that, but more were than I ever suspected. These are the spots where you can net trout as big as beavers on streams you previously hadn't thought much of: trout that can make even the salty head scientist momentarily lose it.

It's possible to go back to that cut with a fly rod a day or two later, run into some other people from the same crew and all get sheepish together. It does feel a little like cheating, but how could you see a huge trout, even under the auspices of a scientific population study, and not go back and try to catch it?

It's not surprising to find the best fish in the undercut bend pools because even small pools can have everything a trout could ask for. The riffle above is a small bug factory providing food, while the pool itself is top-notch cover. The slower current in the bend means the fish doesn't have to work too hard. Of course, he will work on occasion, when it's worth the trouble. During a good hatch a trout may ease out of his undercut to lie at the tail of the riffle, eating bugs. If a grasshopper falls into the water, the fish will charge out after him. He may even use the riffle for spawning, but most of the time he'll lie along that cut bank—maybe just up under it or, better for the fisherman, just out from it a little. You may never see him. All it takes is a flick of the tail and he's several feet back under the bank cuddled up in the old rotting willow roots where nothing but an otter or a fisheries biologist can get at him.

Except for the odd foray, he may stay there his whole life. A. K. once told me about a sixteen-inch two-tone brown he caught from a cut bank on a small stream in Michigan. It was colored like a regular brown trout on the side facing the open stream, but the other side, the one facing the undercut, was an almost chocolate brown. It must take a long time—years—for that to happen.

Also, don't assume that good trout live only in enormous, roomy undercuts. All it takes to hide the fish that can make your day is a slot big enough to stuff a football into.

I don't always fish bend pools in the most efficient way, but when I do, here's how I try to proceed: First, I'll approach it from the inside of the bend. This is where you want to be in terms of casting position, and you also must stay off the bank above the undercut. The trout can hear you coming a block away over there. Remember, this is a little stream, and with so much of the flow concentrated along that far bank, it won't be very wide here. So stay low, with your shadow off the water and all that.

I'll try to come in at, or a little above, the riffle and crouch there for a few minutes looking for rises. If there are some bugs on the water, the fish are most likely to be nosing into the current right where it begins to slow at the head of the pool or maybe just off the main current to the inside. Some of the fish, that is. Even during a good hatch, the big one may well stay back in the pool, eating the flies that drift so close to the bank they brush their wings on the overhanging grass. These guys can be hard to spot.

Another good place is at the tail of the pool where the bottom begins to get shallow again and the current starts to pick up as it slides toward the next riffle.

Once I've spotted the rising fish, I'll pick what I think is the biggest one and deliver a long downstream drift to him with what I think is the appropriate dry fly. I'm in a good position here because even though I'm probably a few feet back from the near bank, casting from my knees, there's an open meadow behind me for the backcast.

If I don't think there *is* a big one, or if I'm just not in my best predatory mood, I'll fish the riffle starting close and working out. If it's a decent-sized stream, I might get two or even three before spooking the pool. On smaller water, I figure one fish caught anywhere in it will spook the whole thing.

Once again, I'm being extreme to make a point, assuming we're on the smallest of streams with the most sensitive of fish. In fact, only two weeks ago on a bend pool that was about thirty yards long and no more than six or eight yards wide, three of us fished a Blue-Winged Olive hatch for over an hour and hooked trout more or less regularly for the whole time. The sky was lightly overcast and the light was flat, which helps. The hatch was heavy enough that the fish were out in the faster water, and that helps, too. Trout don't seem to be able to see out of a riffle as well as they can out of smoother water, and the broken surface helps to hide your leader.

The trout were also really onto the bugs, and they'll sometimes put aside some of their usual caution when they're in an intense feeding mode.

In other words, we were lucky that day, although we naturally took it for skill at the time.

Pile Casting

This is probably a good place to mention the good old pile cast. A standard problem in stream fishing, and an all-time classic on bend pools, is conflicting currents. The trout you want to cast to is lying within inches of the far bank. The current there is very slow, even though the current you're casting across is pretty swift. Anyone who has spent even a single day on a trout stream knows what happens: You cast to the rising fish in the slack current, but the faster flow away from the bank grabs your line and rips it downstream. The fly follows, leaving a wake behind it, and the trout thinks, "I don't know what that was, but I think I'll go hide for an hour on general principles."

The pile cast is just what it sounds like. It piles the leader up so that the fly will float there naturally for the seconds it takes for the current to take up the slack. You do it by straightening the cast beyond where you want the fly to land and then dropping your casting arm, which pulls the leader back to land in a pile with the fly somewhere in the general vicinity.

It sounds sloppy, and it is unless you do it on purpose.

In the worst spots you may get only a two- or three-bob float before the fly motorboats downstream. If you cast downstream, you get a few more seconds because the line has to drift farther to get below the fly. If you can mend the downstream belly in the line back upstream, you can get yet a second or two more. Every cast is different, but if you can get a ten-bob float across fast water in the close quarters of a small stream, you're a world-class pile caster.

You have to learn this and it's not a cast you can easily practice on the lawn. You need current. You also need fish to see the hook-setting problems you'll have with all that slack line.

If you like, you can also run a weighted nymph through that same bend pool. In the deepest darkest ones where no fish are rising, this seems like the logical choice. I like to roll-cast the nymph into the riffle and let it tumble down into the pool because that's what most of the naturals are doing. The closer you are to the hole, the better in terms of drift, while the farther away you are, the better in terms of not spooking the fish. It's a toss-up.

Maybe that's another reason I like the dry fly so much on small streams: given half a break, you can fish it from farther away.

Willows

At the upper end of the meadow, before you get back into the trees again, there's a thick stretch of willows. You know, the kind that are head high or a little taller and packed together so tightly you'd have to crawl on your hands and knees to get through them on shore. The fisherman's trail will do one of three things here. It will swing out around the brush to come back to the stream higher up, it will turn into the stream because the only way to proceed is in the water, or it will stop cold because this is where everyone turns around and goes back.

The stream here is straighter. It doesn't meander as

much because the willows have the banks tied down securely. Those reinforced banks won't be undercut as deeply, either, but they will be undercut some and there will be some very cozy places for trout to lie. If it's in the Rocky Mountains it's probably shallow and pebbly on the bottom. If it's in a Michigan swamp it may be slower and deeper with a gooey clay bottom, and there are lots of gradations in between. Whatever, streams in willow thickets can be very fishy.

More than anything, this is a casting problem. The specific conditions will dictate whether it's rated as a minor annoyance, a screaming rod breaker, or somewhere in between.

When the willows are low and scattered, as they'll often be where you move from the meadow into the thicket, you're probably just looking at keeping your backcast high and glancing over your shoulder regularly to see where it's going.

A little farther on, the bushes are taller and closer together. Now you're watching your line on every backcast, trying to keep it in what seems like the one open slot in fifty square miles and are, in fact, beginning to roll-cast more.

Still farther on, the willows get absolutely luxurious. Dozens of thin trunks sprout from every root. They lean out over the stream until it looks like it's flowing through a tunnel. It's shady and cool in here and the trout may be involved in what amounts to a day-long evening rise. It's simultaneously some of the best trout habitat on the stream and some of the worst casting.

The roll cast is the only one that works now, and even at that it has to be low and tight-looped. If you're an average caster like me, you can work the middle of the stream, but the overhanging root-bound banks where the big fish like to lie begin to get seriously problematic. You'd pay ten dollars for the room to make one sidearm cast so you could flip a dry fly along that delicious-looking bank.

A crisp, low, sidearm roll cast is something I've been working on and I can now do it on a fairly regular basis as long as I don't try for too much distance. You *will* learn to roll-cast on willowy creeks if only to save yourself those long sweaty climbs into the bushes to retrieve your flies. With a bad roll cast, your fly will be hooked conveniently in your hat.

In the toughest willow tunnels some resort to the bow-and-arrow cast. That's where you hold the fly between thumb and forefinger—*behind the point of the hook*—and shoot it to the target using the rod as a bow. It does work, but I'll have a ways to go before I perfect it. My main problem is accuracy. I can get the fly out there, but I hang it up on something at least half the time.

That's not peculiar to the bow-and-arrow cast, of course. On brushy streams it's as easy to snag yourself on the forward cast as on the backcast. Then you're faced with the age-old decision: do you break the fly off, tie on a new one and try it again, or do you go and get it?

It's up to you.

Now. So far we've been fishing this brushy stretch upstream because that's the convenient way to get around in there. It's actually a lot easier to deliver your fly from upstream, but that involves many trips into the willows where your face will get slapped and your fly line will get tangled.

Roll casting in a willow tunnel.

But just for the sake of argument, let's say you've spotted a trout you guess to be sixteen or seventeen inches long lying under some overhanging willows. You'd like to be able to deliver a tight roll cast with a little left-handed hook in the last twelve inches of leader, but, the longer you look at it, the more your confidence fades. This has suddenly leaped upward from an interesting little casting problem to a fish you really want to catch.

What you want to do here is get out of the stream, walk around, and come in well above the fish. From here you can roll-cast your fly to the current tongue that will take it right to the fish and then feed slack line with the long downstream drift for a perfect drag-free float. If he doesn't take it on the first try, let the cast swing out below him and retrieve it slowly back along the far bank.

You can do that effectively with a streamer, too, although you'll want to keep the line tight to give the fly a little swimming action and so you can feel the strike. On a rising trout, or even one that's holding near the surface, I'll use the dry. The streamer I'll reserve for a fishy-looking spot where I can't actually see a trout, but where one ought to be. I figure he'll move for the streamer if he wants it while he may not even see the little dry fly unless I accidently put it in just the right spot.

The hardest part of this is getting out on the bank and scrabbling through those willows. If I knew the secret to this I'd tell you. All I can suggest is, stay calm and don't expect to make great time.

And don't wander off too far looking for an easy route and lose the stream. I did that once and came very close to getting pissed off.

Willow tunnels can get very tough. I've seen a few small creeks where the overhanging branches were only a few feet above the water, where you actually *had* to fish a streamer on a tight line because you couldn't see the spot you were fishing to. The specific place I'm thinking of was further confused by regular logjams that sectioned the stream off into beautifully deep—but also nearly impossible to reach—pools.

I hooked some good trout in there by feeding in a streamer with a split-shot on its nose to sink it. I'd fish the first pool, then wade down to the logjam and drift the fly into the next one from there. The fish were browns and they were unusually easy to hook, no doubt because they were hardly ever fished for.

I say "hooked" because I never did actually land a fish. There wasn't even room to cast in any civilized way, so I'd just hold the fly in my left hand and toss it into the water. There was also no room to use the rod to play a fish and I lost several while just sitting there thinking this would be a hell of a lot easier with a hand line. I don't consider myself a purist, but I do like to use a rod of some kind.

I guess the point here is, there really are some places that are unfishable for one reason or another, although there aren't very many that aren't at least worth a try. It's not universally true that the biggest trout live in the hardest spots to fish, but it's true often enough.

The Forest Stream

Farther upstream the willows begin to give way to real trees and you're in a forest. The gradient is a little steeper here, and the stream is faster. There are some odd features here and there, including some larger rocks, but mostly it's a long marginal riffle that occasionally breaks into a fast pool.

There are those who will pass this water by, or fish it very spottily, casting only to the few holes and maybe along the deeper banks. There's no doubt those are the best places, but I'm constantly surprised where trout can come from in water like this. It's actually much better habitat than it looks like at first glance.

The faster water flowing over the textured bottom is richly aerated and the streambed itself, with all that surface area, will harbor more insects than just about any other bottom type. The place has a little more structure than a true riffle—which is a bit more uniform—and so there's also some holding water for the trout.

Now I don't think trout live in places like this on a year-round basis, but they move into them to feed. A fish will find a little bit of slack water to hold in and from that vantage point he'll pick off the bugs, floating and otherwise, that come past. He may spend the day in there or just move in during the mornings and evenings when the light is low. If there's not much bug activity, the trout may not venture into the faster water at all, but stay down below where the stream is quieter and deeper. During something like a heavy hatch they may charge up into the fastest, shallowest water under the bright noonday sun, apparently figuring it's better to eat when the food is there than to be shy and cautious.

Some holding spots will be obvious. A basketball-sized rock midcurrent will make a little eddy behind it big enough for a good-sized fish to lie in comfortably. A crease or dip in the bottom will make a quiet slot that can hold a couple of trout. Spots like that are easy to see and you'll naturally put a few casts over each one.

But don't stop there. I had to catch a lot of trout from unlikely places before I started to realize that *no place* is completely unlikely on a trout stream. Even in an ankle-deep, uniformly fast riffle, the hydrology is cryptic. All it takes is a tiny glitch in the bottom structure to make a dead spot where a trout can lounge all day without batting a fin.

I can seldom spot fish in water like this. Now and then I'll see one rise, especially if he's doing it regularly, and sometimes I'll see what I think is the flash of a fish under the surface, but mostly I'm just not sure. So I cast to it anyway. On the days when I'm hot, it's gratifying how often I'm right. A. K. has had the same experience. He says you should proceed on the assumption that if you think you saw a trout, you probably did.

I guess what I actually end up doing is casting at least once or twice to everything but the genuine white water, just to see what will happen. I'll usually work upstream because that way I can manage a fairly short cast and still get good drifts.

This is pleasant fishing and also graduate-level casting practice. Good drifts can be really tricky in all those fast, conflicting currents and, because you're never really sure where the trout will be, every one you screw up could have cost you a fish.

Of course, you can fish the same stretch by casting downstream if you want—in fact, you'll probably get better drifts with a dry fly that way—but you'll have to make longer casts. I make my decision based on nothing more mysterious than where I've parked the truck and whether I'm going in or coming out.

If I *am* fishing downstream, and the dry fly isn't exactly knocking them dead, I'll sometimes go to a streamer. I'll usually put a split-shot right on the fly's nose to get it down deep and wiggle it around in the riffle sort of feeling for the holding spots. I'll try to fish it straight downstream so I can pump it gently in the water like a little fish struggling in the current.

As I said, streamers are more effective in small streams than some people think, and they have the added advantage that in especially tight spots (or on especially lazy days) you can fish a single cast for twenty minutes.

Pocket Water

Somewhere in here, the marginal riffle will become true pocket water. The stream is still fairly swift— maybe even a little faster than before because the gradient has increased—and now it's all jumbled up with boulders. It's the place on a small stream where you have every kind of structure you'll find on a big river, only in miniature: fast slots, glides, riffles, pools—everything I've mentioned up to now and then some. It's a tight, complex hydrological situation with lots of holding water for trout and good habitat for insects.

Casting may or may not be difficult here, depending on what the bankside cover is like, but your real problems will have to do with fly drag. I mentioned conflicting currents earlier, but that was nothing compared to what you'll find in pocket water. As the name implies, there will be small pockets of slow water against a backdrop of fast, sinuous current. In some places there will be eddies: small-scale backwaters where two currents lying right next to each other will be going in opposite directions.

The trout will usually lie on the edges of such things, the places where they can be in the slowest water that's still near the fast water that's carrying the food. Among other things, this means the trout won't all be facing one way. They'll probably be lying with their noses into the current as usual, but that current coils around so much that what we think of as upstream and downstream (in our rather simplistic way) tends to be meaningless. In a nice, churning section of pocket water, the trout are likely to be facing every which way.

This can make approaching the water unseen a little touchy, but you actually get a couple of breaks here. For one thing, much of the water will be fast and broken with small holding spots scattered around in it. A given trout, or even a small pod of them, will be holding in what amounts to a tiny self-contained bit of habitat: maybe a few square feet behind a midcurrent rock where a little slick eddy lies along a tongue of almost white water. The rest of the stream, out there past all the rocks and bubbles, will be lost to this trout, and because of the rough surface he won't be able to see out very well, either.

The point is, the fish's visibility is very limited in pocket water and you can get surprisingly close to him without his knowing about it—given, naturally, a modicum of caution on your part. Chances are good that you'll spook some other fish on the way to the trout in question, but you get a break there, too. A frightened trout dives for the nearest cover, and in pocket water that's often just inches away.

A trout spooked in a wide, open, smooth glide will sometimes charge through the whole pool on his way to the specific rock or cut bank he wants to hide in. His colleagues understand that this means trouble and scatter like flushed quail. There's a long pool right across from the house here where that happens on a regular basis, especially in late summer and fall when the water is down. It's funny how much you can get to like a stretch of water you haven't hooked a trout in for two years running. In pocket water, however, a spooked fish will often just slip under the nearest rock without disturbing the rest of the run.

Then again, you'll sometimes get a panicky fish who'll dart through every piece of holding water in sight like a fast rat through a familiar maze. This is most likely to happen on the smallest creeks, but can happen anywhere. It's the breaks.

You can get a fair idea of how little the fish can see in pocket water by noticing how little *you* can see. I can spot fish under these conditions, but my best guess is I see one for every dozen, and half of them have clearly seen me first. So, I fish the water again, running many well-considered drifts through what I take to be the most likely places, concentrating on current edges, with a few odd casts to everyplace else for good measure.

I like a dry fly for pocket water because you stand a better chance of being able to see how the drift is going and to spot the strikes, although it's possible to miss seeing both.

This low-visibility business—both yours and the

trout's—works both ways. You can sometimes get nice and close to the spot you want to fish in pocket water because the fish can't see out too well. Fine, but on the other hand, your casts have to be very accurate. For example: There lies a fat, foot-long brook trout. He's behind a rock, in an eddy the size of a hubcap. The main current is flowing straight east, while the backwater turns around and flows pretty much west. The trout lies there in two feet of almost dead water, looking east by southeast, waiting for something good to eat to come along.

A fly dropped behind him in the eddy will be out of his line of sight. Worse yet, a small fish may take it and blow the whole thing for you. The same fly drifted past him as little as six inches into that fast current may also be out of his view; either that or he just doesn't want to swim out there to get it. He'll wait for one to come closer.

Ideally, the fly should go by right in the crease. It should dance, not knowing whether to follow the heavy water or drift into the eddy. The trout will like that. There the bug is if he wants it, but it's on its way past, too, so if he *does* want it he has to take it right now. Enough time to grasp the situation, but not enough to think it over too much.

Okay, trout probably don't really think in those terms but, luckily, they have outdoor writers to think for them.

That, as I said, is the ideal cast, but others will work. Let's take that same spot, but make the fast current more like a glide. It's not as much work for the fish to dart out there now, and he can see farther into it, too, so you may be able to get away with running the fly past him out in the main current. If you're casting from the right place—say, across and a little upstream on the fast-water side—it's a much easier drift, one you can make again and again, more or less perfectly, until the fish is convinced.

If he's not convinced after a while—and not spooked, either—you can then try the harder drift right in the crease, the cast that has to be somewhere between pretty damned good and perfect the first time.

In this same spot, where the main current is slower and the back current is less severe, the fish might not be looking so singlemindedly at that one strip of current. He might, in fact, be nosing around in the eddy, in which case a fly that drifts lazily in the slick water could be the one he's looking for.

All of these casts can be tricky and, as much as I've searched over the years, there doesn't seem to be a workable substitute for well-practiced casting skills. Still, the closer you can get, the easier these kinds of drifts are. The less line you have on the water, the less drag you'll get, and you'll also be in more direct contact with line and leader for mending.

In the tightest spots with the most wildly conflicting currents, you may want to have only a few inches of leader actually on the water, and at some point in there you're dapping rather than actually casting.

Dapping is where you use nothing but the rod tip and a few feet of leader to simply "place" the fly on the surface. In its purest form, nothing but the fly itself touches the water, although in practice it's seldom as tidy as that. Naturally this eliminates any and all drag problems and makes deadly accuracy a breeze to pull off, but getting that close and holding the rod tip right over the fish can blow your cover.

Dapping works best for me in tight pocket water with lots of fast current and, with luck, a bush or a nice big rock for me to hide behind.

Another advantage to dapping is that it lets you put some subtle and very realistic-looking action on the fly. This can be very effective and sometimes spells the difference between a cautious inspection from a trout and a confident take.

Fly Action

I think there are only two things to remember when it comes to putting action on a dry fly: first, bugs are weaker than kittens and their hops and twitches are feeble; second, an insect struggling against the current is doing just that, struggling *against* the current—whatever slight movements he makes will almost always be in an upstream direction. That means that, unless you're one of the flashiest fly casters alive, you'll want to be drifting the fly downstream so you can twitch it back up.

In rare cases the action on the fly can be vigorous— cases involving unusually wild, eager fish and/or something like a blanket hatch of big caddis in a high wind. Then you can skitter a bushy fly six inches across the current and still get strikes. But don't count on it. Usually a light touch is best.

All things being equal, I'll try the good old dead drift first in most situations and then go to a gentle twitch if that doesn't work, but sometimes the clues from the stream are just too obvious to ignore. If there are big mayflies jumping around on the water, or maybe a swarm of bumbling caddisflies, I'll go to the worked fly right off. It's not always the right choice, but the possibility of skipping basic steps and going right to The Answer is too tempting for someone with a low tolerance for spadework.

And, yes, you can use all these pocket-water techniques with a weighted nymph, too. The only significant difference will be that strikes will be harder to detect. In fact, nymphing is probably the most effective method in streams where the water is more than a couple of feet deep, or even in shallower creeks on those days when the trout just aren't looking up.

As with dry flies, I'll try the dead drift first with a nymph, but there are times when a little action is better. I like the old Leisenring Lift, where you let the fly sink to the bottom and then raise it gently with the fly rod to mimic a nymph or pupa swimming toward the surface. I like this because you have more control and usually a better hooking angle, too.

Another method is to sink the fly, let it drift downstream, and simply allow the weight of the current against the leader to lift it off the bottom. This is one many of us discovered by mistake; the dead drift wasn't working, but we started getting strikes at the end of the drift, right when we began to lift the fly for another cast. Ah ha! we thought, and started doing it on purpose.

There are those who'll tell you that you'll regularly take larger trout if you fish nymphs rather than dry flies, but I haven't found that to be true on small streams. I've even gone so far as to test this by fishing the same well-known stretch of creek with dry flies and nymphs on alternate days without noticing a significant difference in either size or numbers of fish. I think it's more accurate to say that some spots (like deep, dark plunge pools) are best fished with split-shot and a nymph, while others (like glides, riffles, and shallow pocket water) are better dry-fly water.

Special Situations

What all this amounts to is a simplified view of a fairly typical small trout stream: a handful each of water types and fishing methods, both of which have more variations than you'll be able to see in a lifetime of fly fishing. And scattered around in there will be all sorts of special situations.

Beaver ponds could use a book all to themselves. At the risk of oversimplifying it, you fish them as you would a lake, paying special attention to the inlet and outlet where the current collects insects, which, in turn, collect trout. The water in front of the dam is often very good. As the current begins to pick up there, it will sooner or later transport every floating bug on the pond through a fairly narrow slot, and the fish who lie there have the tangled sticks of the dam to dive into for cover.

An excellent way to fish a beaver pond is from below the dam where the only parts of you that are exposed to view are your hat and your rod. From here you can fish out in a pattern with progressively longer casts and, on a small pond at least, cover a good half of the water. Another advantage is that even in heavy cover you'll have the open stream channel behind you for a clear backcast.

The one drawback here is that your line *will* get tangled in the dam—no question about it—and it will probably happen at a very inopportune moment. I try to keep my loose line in loops held in my left hand while I cast with my right, but if you can cast and retrieve for half an hour and never drop that line, you have more concentration than I do.

Between the line, the sticks, the sucking current, and your own big feet, a snag can take fifteen minutes to fix. But then, nothing is perfect.

Except when fish are rising well, I'll usually fish a beaver pond with something like a soft-hackled wet fly or maybe a small leech-style streamer, using a slow crawling hand-twist retrieve. I put at least a little bit of weight on the shanks of these things when I tie them and, when fishing shallow water or working close to the banks, I'll generally fish them just like that. A lightly weighted fly will not sink too deeply of its own weight because it will be buoyed up by the floating leader, but that's okay when the spot you're fishing is fairly shallow. In deeper water I'll add a little lead to the leader, which works well enough, although it does deaden the feel a little on subtle strikes.

In a beaver pond that's regularly deeper than, let's say, five feet, a medium sink-tip line with a short leader is probably the best way to go, but I think a beaver pond, and a big, deep one at that, is the only place where you'll need a sinking line of any kind on a small stream. I seldom carry a sink-tip line on a small stream unless a lake is also on the program.

And while we're on this, don't forget the stream channels between beaver ponds. They're often slow and deep with good trout in them and they're usually ignored by fishermen who eagerly charge from one pond to the next.

Pay special attention to sloughs and backwater.

Now and then you'll come upon other still-water situations on small streams: a huge pool in the main
channel, maybe, or a big swampy backwater. I always
try to fish these systematically because trout can't be
counted on to be in any particular place in still water;
they'll cruise around.

As with beaver ponds, you fish these like lakes,
keeping in mind that the scale is vastly reduced.
Always explore structures that involve different kinds
of habitat than the rest of the stream, especially
those where the water gets calm or unusually deep.
You may have to re-rig from the way you've been
fishing (maybe changing from a dry fly to a little
streamer) and put a serious sneak on the spot, but it's
not unusual to find a couple of larger than normal
trout in places like that.

Plunge pools of all kinds can be just great, not only
because they're good feeding spots, but because a
pool that's been chewed out to some depth by falling
water may be the only place for miles on a small creek
where a trout can live through enough winters to get
real big. I love it when I come to a deep plunge where
no fish are rising, not even a few little ones at the tail.
I take it to mean that the one fish who *does* live there
has eaten up all the rest and is still hungry.

Take that same plunge pool, tip the gradient up a
little more, and you have a tub fed by a modest water-
fall. If there's one of these in your neighborhood, I'll
bet you twenty dollars it's called "The Tub." This is
also potential big-trout habitat on a small stream.
The main problem is, kids will like to swim in it.

Another dandy pool is the one backed up by a logjam—good current, deep water, and a whole labyrinth

of old waterlogged timber for trout to hide in. As with all pools, curiosity can get you to dredging it deeply with a weighted nymph or streamer. Fish it close to the sticks and don't be surprised if you lose a fly or two.

Weed beds—the thicker the better—are a fabulous thing to see in a small stream. They say "spring creek," or something close to it: water that's very rich. Aquatic vegetation is pasture for insects, crustaceans, and sometimes even baitfish, all of which make trout fat. The stream plants you hear about most are watercress and elodea but, frankly, I have never gotten into the botany of it. All I know is, weeds are good. Based on my experience, you're probably looking at some hefty trout that will be hard to catch because of the abundant food supply—which stifles a trout's natural curiosity—and the thick cover that makes them hard to land once hooked.

Most thickly weeded streams are slow-flowing and smooth, so on rising trout you'll need long casts, good long drifts, and possibly even very fine leaders that are easily broken when the hooked fish dives into the vegetation (or "crap" as it's often called in these situations).

Nymphing can be trickier yet, with all the problems of dry-fly fishing plus the need to get close. But, for those fat fish who spend almost all their time grazing lazily on sow bugs or freshwater shrimp in the deep water, you'll have to try it. It's either that or wait for the cosmic hatch, which may not come off every day, or even every week.

In addition, a genuine spring creek may require some more-than-usually accurate fly patterns and, if it's well known and heavily fished, as many are, the trout can be insanely cautious and selective. I think it's fair to say that spring creeks are noticeably different (more difficult, that is) than your regular old trout creek, but they are still best fished in the same way: with stealth and long drifts.

The Civilized Stream

So far, this small stream we've been looking at has been flowing through forests, meadows, and canyons: lonely, wild, solitary, quiet, and, in case I haven't mentioned it, heartbreakingly beautiful. It's not just a device. The ones I'm thinking of are actually like that, which is why I used them in the first place. I've been having a great time sitting here picturing some of my favorite stretches of creek and talking about how I've fished them—even if I don't always do it as well in person as I do in print.

But some small streams are more civilized, and those can be good, too. They have retaining walls, rip-rapped banks, irrigation dams, head gates, and bridges on them. Some even flow, complete with trout, through small towns—past the fire station, through a couple of backyards, and on into Old Man So-and-So's field.

Man-made structures don't usually fit into the fisherman's preconceived aesthetic program (with the notable exception of covered bridges) but they are not to be ignored.

An irrigation dam with a head gate into a ditch off to one side may not be the prettiest thing you've ever seen on a small trout stream, but it can be a good place to fish. The dam will back up a nice pool ahead of it and may make a good plunge pool below. The biggest trout ever seen on the creek across the street was an eight-pound brown. He came from beneath the undercut cement abutment below an irrigation dam—a pool that becomes a lot prettier once you know what lives in it.

Stone retaining walls are placed to keep the stream from eating away a bank, but the stream is persistent and tends to eat out under it a little bit anyway, making a sheltered spot where trout like to hide. There's one across the street where, in August, a grasshopper fly will almost always draw a strike or two. It's an old wall, and old ones are usually the best.

Riprapped banks along roads also provide cover that's worth fishing, although in many cases it's not as good as the natural cover they destroyed. Most streams would be better off without roads along them, but as long as the roads are there, you might as well catch a few trout.

Bridges provide the shade trout love; their pilings can amount to extra cover, and they'll often constrict the current enough to carve out a nice hole. It's usually known locally as "The Bridge Pool."

What we're looking at here is probably not the prettiest stretch of small trout stream you've ever seen, one you'll never see on the cover of a magazine. On the other hand, it *is* a trout stream, and it might even have a card up its sleeve. There are a lot of other fishermen who don't think it's all that pretty, either, and many of them will drive right past it on their way to the headwaters in the National Forest. I know of at least two creeks that give up their best fly fishing within the limits of the towns they flow through simply because these stretches are not what you'd call scenic and so are not very heavily fished.

I usually don't mind the lack of scenery too much except on those days when pine forests and snow-capped mountains are more important than fish. In fact, I have tremendous respect for any human settlement that, in this day and age, still has a working trout stream flowing through it. If nothing else, it's a town you can feel at home in.

You Can Catch 'Em on Anything

I actually do have a small-stream fly selection that's different from the bulging-vest total-assault program I use on big rivers, and every winter, in the course of tying the next season's trout flies, I stop to fiddle with it. For a while I had the whole thing in a single box with covered compartments and clips in the lid, one of those things designed for the fly fisherman who has just the one box. I liked that. With one fly box and a handful of odds and ends (clippers, forceps, a tube of fly floatant, split-shot, a few spools of leader material) I could fish the local creeks without a vest. I pictured myself as light, mobile, unencumbered—a fly-fishing guerrilla.

Then, gradually, the selection escalated to two, and finally three, boxes as I began to see the old "you can catch 'em on anything" business as the myth it was. Most who said that didn't really mean you can catch 'em on anything, but "We don't really care if we catch 'em at all. I mean, it's just a creek, right?"

I don't want to say I decided to take small-stream fishing "seriously"—that seems like the wrong word in this context—but I think I decided to give it the respect it deserved. These are trout streams, after all, the places where tweedy types stand around rooting through fly boxes for the right pattern.

At this writing, one of two things has happened: either the small-stream selection has shrunk back

down to one box or I've managed to develop two separate batches of flies, one for small streams in general,
and another for the few I fish all the time and know well
enough to feel confident about.

The Core Selection

The one-box selection is the core—the flies I would
not go fishing without any more than I'd go hunting
without bullets. It no longer assumes that you can
catch them on anything, but operates on the suspicion
that you might be able to catch them most of the time
if you cover your bets.

The main dry fly here is the Adams, that wonderfully
buggy, suggestive, nondescript Michigan pattern that,
based on sales, is America's favorite fly. In fast water,
low light, or on streams where the fish just aren't all
that picky, an Adams in the right size has been known
to pass for just about any winged aquatic insect. I like
to carry them in sizes 10 or 12 down through 20 to cover
the board.

In more tightly focused situations (again in the right
size) it will sometimes properly imitate any number of
dark mayflies, from Blue Duns to Hendricksons and,
in a pinch, will pass for some of the light ones as well.
For example, I've occasionally done well fishing a #12
Adams as a Green Drake.

The Adams also works well as a searching or generic
bug pattern, the one you can use to pound up curious
trout that aren't already rising. It also works as a caddis
pattern, which, I've been told, is what Len Halliday in-
tended it to be when he invented it. According to the
story, the original pattern had down-wings, like a cad-
disfly, but as it became more popular, and more professional tiers got their hands on it, the wings gradually

cocked up into the traditional mayfly configuration we see now.

Authentic or not, there's just something magical about it that fish like, although I've never heard anyone explain the phenomenon to my satisfaction. Still, if someone tells me a stretch of small stream is "Adams water," I know exactly what they mean.

I guess I love the Adams for the same reasons everyone else does: it's a proven fish catcher and an item of tradition, two things it's hard to ignore. In fact, there are places where, if you don't have at least a few of these flies in your box, fishermen will frown and ask you where the hell you're from and game wardens will call in your fishing license to see if there are any warrants out on you.

Caddisflies are a staple trout food on many small streams around the country and, since silhouette is second in importance only to size, you should have some kind of down-wing pattern.

I like the Elk Hair Caddis, and so do a lot of other people. It's simple, easy to tie, a good floater, and a fair impressionistic rendering of one of the most common trout stream insects. I carry them in sizes 12 through 16 or 18 to cover most of our local caddisflies. They've also been known to adequately copy other down-wing bugs like small stoneflies and large midges.

I like to have a light one and a dark one. The light one is known locally as the St. Vrain Caddis, although it appears around the country under other names. It has a pale yellow dubbed body, blond elk-hair wing, and a ginger hackle. The dark one has an olive body, tan elk wing, and a mixed brown-and-grizzly hackle like the Adams. When fishing a hatch I match light or dark flies to the shade of the bugs on the water. When I use a caddis as a search pattern I use the one I can see the best under the lighting conditions of the moment. Usually it's the light one.

For summer and early fall fishing just about anywhere in the country, you'll want a good grasshopper pattern. I like the A. K. Best Hopper because I like A. K., but also because it nicely splits the difference between two types. It's dressed heavily enough—complete with clipped deer-hair head and palmer hackle—to be a good floater for fast water, but it's also trim enough to pass in slower currents.

Ant patterns are easy—just a couple bumps of dubbing with a few turns of hackle in between—and they're very effective small-stream flies in the summer. If you've ever bothered to look, you'll know that there are zillions of ants everywhere—probably more ants than any other single creature on the planet. And trout like them. What a break. I carry a black and a cinnamon pattern in sizes 14 through 20, or thereabouts.

Some kind of tiny midge dry fly is a must, I think, especially late in the season. These little two-winged aquatic flies are common on every trout stream I can think of. They aren't often the hatch that accounts for the frantic feeding activity associated with larger bugs, and they make a poor search pattern, but they fill in the gaps in the trout's diet left between the more impressive hatches, and when fish are onto midges they often won't look at anything else.

Once again, I like to have a light and a dark fly. The cream midge has a body of tan thread, a wing of creamy-colored pheasant quill (from the secondary wing feather), and a very sparse ginger hackle. The black midge has a black thread body, black hackle, and a white duck-quill wing. I carry them starting at size

20—overlapping my smallest Adams—down to as small as I felt like making them the winter before. I've gone as little as a 28, but have stopped short of the 32. And, frankly, I still have some of the first #28 dry flies I ever tied. If the trout are selective to #28 midges, chances are good that I'll surrender.

Midges are often considered to be specialty patterns, not something everyone would carry on a small stream, but there have been days when they made a real difference, and making the difference is what a fly selection is all about.

Another pattern in that same class is the mayfly spinner. This fly anticipates the same kind of situation that's created by the midge hatch: the thing that doesn't happen all that often, but that you, by God, have to have the right pattern for when it does.

It's a matter of the proper silhouette again. When the adult mating mayflies fall spent on the water, the trout will get on them, both because there are lots of them and because they're easy targets, being somewhere between dying and dead and not likely to take off again. You can have a dry fly that's the right size and the right color, but if it doesn't have a long tail and spent wings, you'll encounter many trout who aren't interested.

There was a time when I carried only the Chocolate Spinner. This has split tails of dun hackle fibers, a body of chocolate-colored dubbing, and spent light-dun wings: a classic dark spinner pattern. My theory on spinners lined up something like this: Next to size, silhouette is the most important element of any fly pattern, and a spinner fly is *pure* silhouette. The vast majority of the spinner falls I've seen have been in the evening or in the low light of an overcast late afternoon. Under these conditions a dark fly is considered best because it cuts a cleaner outline against the sky than a light one does. Or, if you prefer it in terms of the old fly-fishing proverb: Dark day, dark fly.

It still sounds good, and like all angling theories—even wrong ones—it works part of the time. But there were just too many evenings when trout rising to light bugs, like the spinners of the Pale Morning Duns and *Callibaetis* mayflies, were suspicious of the dark flies.

So, I backed the Chocolate Spinners up with some cream ones, both in sizes 12 through 20, and added a footnote to the theory to the effect that the dark fly doesn't work when the naturals are light because the dark spinner cuts a sharp outline while the naturals *don't*.

I also like to have a candy-store dry fly—also known as an attractor pattern—because they work, even though no one seems to know why. My favorite is the good old Royal Wulff with its red-floss joint, gobs of green peacock herl, and easy to see white hairwings. It's a version of the fabled Royal Coachman and it is, I think, a real milestone in this area; that is, an improvement on an old pattern that really *is* an improvement. It's just as good as the Coachman, but it's more durable, more visible, and it floats better. If you put all of Lee Wulff's other accomplishments aside, he'd still have a firm place in history for this one fly pattern, just as Len Halliday has for the Adams.

And no, I don't have any idea how or why it works, but it fits in nicely with the other half of that old fishing saw, which says: Bright day, bright fly. I will say it delights me no end that you can catch trout on something like this because it puts some of the playfulness back into a sport that has gotten pretty scientific lately.

I guess what I'm trying to say is, not only do I not know why it works, I don't *want* to know.

Interestingly enough, size can make a difference with attractor patterns. It's not usually a real hairsplitter, but a 16 can be better than a 20, and a 12 can outfish a 16. More than anything, it seems to have to do with water type; a #20 Royal Wulff may be all it takes to pique a trout's curiosity in slow shallow water, while you might need a #12 to draw attention in a fast riffle.

The Royal Wulff is one of the flies I don't tie well, especially in the smaller sizes, so I've been known to buy them, even though it's almost a point of honor with me to tie my own flies. I stock up on them when I go to Montana because up there the Royal Wulff is the state bird and the flies are tied especially well.

I like the Hare's Ear Soft Hackle for a wet fly. Many consider this to be a caddis pupa imitation, and it works well for that, but it also functions as an all-around subsurface bug for searching and will sometimes pass for just about any nymphal or larval form. It also works well as a mayfly emerger, even though it's not what most of us picture when we think of that kind of pattern.

To me, the Hare's Ear Soft Hackle is up there with the Adams as a favorite pattern of all time. If you count it as a standard variation of the old-time Hare's Ear, it even carries around the same baggage of tradition. If I absolutely had to go fishing with only two flies, they'd be an Adams and a Hare's Ear Soft Hackle, but let's not kid ourselves. Nobody goes fishing with just two flies unless he's secretly using worms or trying to win a bet.

To cover the mayfly nymphs, I like the Pheasant Tail. It's dark—as most mayfly nymphs are—has a realisti-

cally trim abdomen that's still fuzzy enough to suggest
the gills on the naturals, and it's easy to tie. I carry
them in sizes 10 or 12 through 20 and tie them un-
weighted so they can be greased with fly floatant and
used as floating emergers. The floating nymph trick
works so often that now, when rising trout refuse my
dry fly, I'll usually go right to something like a greased
Pheasant Tail fished right in the surface film. During
many mayfly hatches, that, rather than a different dry
fly, is the answer.

I also have a few small midge pupa patterns, just for
good measure: simple little things made with nothing
more than a quill or moose-mane hair body and a
tiny ball of dubbing for the thorax. I seldom actually
nymph-fish with these in small streams, although I
have caught the odd trout on them that way. They are,
in fact, reserved for that single situation where there's a
midge hatch and the trout refuse the dry midge pattern. Then one of these tiny emergers fished in, or a
fraction of an inch under, the surface film is the way to
get strikes.

To be honest, whole seasons go by when I never use a
midge pupa on a creek, and this is probably the one fly
you could take out of the selection without hearing me
scream too loudly. I guess I carry them because I have
the dry midges, which I do find useful, and that sort of
commits me to carrying the pupae in the interest of
entomological integrity. This is an attempt at what fly
fishermen loosely refer to as "logic."

There's some logic to the streamers, too. The Weed-
less Woolly is a cross between the Woolly Bugger and a
marabou streamer, tied upside down on the hook to
make it somewhat snag-proof. It's a leech pattern that's
kind of nasty looking with lots of action, tied in either

black or olive. This one is especially good in slow streams and beaver ponds.

The Bucktail Muddler is what it sounds like, a bucktail version of the standard Muddler Minnow—a big-headed, beefy, sculpin-type streamer with teddy bear eyeballs—that's also tied so that the hook rides up.

If the Woolly is subtle and seductive, the Muddler is a hamburger. Trout who don't like one type will sometimes be tempted by the other.

That's the logic I was talking about. Hope you weren't expecting more.

The other one I like to have along is what I think of as the spawning-trout streamer. It's a standard bucktail with lots of fluorescent orange in the wing, a color that seems to really get spawning fish angry. It's the streamer that, when stripped past a spawning trout, will often get bitten rather than just chased or flashed.

This one also doubles as the gaudy streamer in the selection, the one that will sometimes work when the more drab realistic-looking patterns don't produce. It's a good fly for eager brookies.

I tie all of these streamers upside down in the interests of fewer snags, and I think that's an especially important feature on small streams. A creek may be rocky, brushy, or full of logjams, but whatever it's like, there will be plenty of opportunities to lose flies. And I, for one, can be a lot more daring about casting to sticky spots when I think there's a chance I'll get my fly back.

That, as I said, is the one-box small-stream fly selection. It was assembled in the same way you'd put together a light survival kit: just the basics, no frills, no luxuries, but with most day-to-day problems addressed. With it I'd be willing to try out any small

Traveling light: a two-box fly selection and light bamboo rod.

stream, creek, brook, trickle, or irrigation ditch in the country, figuring I'd have something reasonable to tie on regardless of what was, or wasn't, happening at the moment. Notice I didn't say I'd catch trout, just that I'd have the wherewithal to try.

There are a number of small streams that I fish with just that single box, but I'll be honest with you—they're local creeks where I know from experience that the fish are seldom very selective. Or if they do happen to be picky about fly patterns in the flats, I know there are trout just upstream in the pocket water that will probably eat an Adams.

And they are *local* streams, which means the pressure is off. If I make the twenty-minute drive up to the Middle Fork for a few hours of fishing and get skunked, I don't have days away from work, airline tickets, and an out-of-state license to account for. "It was just nice to get out," I say, and it was.

Naturally, this fly selection is offered "in my humble opinion," a phrase that should appear somewhere in any discussion of something so regional, personal, and maybe even mystical.

I'll stand by the general makeup of the thing, but I won't argue patterns. If you want to use something like a Gray Wulff instead of the Adams, fine. If you want to back that up with a light-colored all-around fly like the Blond Wulff or March Brown, that's fine, too, and also a pretty good idea. As an important element of an effective fly pattern, color (or maybe shade) comes right after size and silhouette.

The Regional Influence

That's personal preference, but there's a strong regional influence, too. For instance, in the small streams around here—one major drainage, two counties—you'll find lots of Red Quill, Blue-Winged Olive, and Ginger Quill mayflies. These are common hatches that you'll see year after year and that are around for a long time on one stretch of stream or another.

There are more than just three species of bug involved here, of course, but it just so happens that those three fly patterns, in a variety of sizes, will cover what I take to be the vast majority of mayfly hatches around the country. There's a reddish brown one, a grayish olive one, and a light cream one. Granted, fly tiers and fishermen will hassle endlessly about subtle shades of color that you can't tell apart at arm's length. I don't want to be the one to say that stuff doesn't matter (and even if it doesn't matter it's still fun) but those three flies, in the right size, will at least suggest most of the mayflies you'll ever run into.

But then, if you live in the Northeast, you'd probably be nuts to fish a small stream without a couple of Quill Gordons, in parts of the mountain West you could be lost without *E. flavilinea* (little green drakes), there are Michigan waters where you'd better have a couple of enormous *Hexagenias* stuck in your hatband (they're too big for most fly boxes, anyway), and I know a Pennsylvania-creek fisherman who wouldn't step out the front door without a couple of Coffin Flies. And so on. Regional preferences are not to be ignored. They are more than just fashion.

Look at terrestrials. I fish mostly hoppers and ants, although now that I'm sliding from the first fly box into the second I have room for a few other things. Flying ants, for example. Flying ant falls are spotty around here, but when they happen they're fabulous, and the regular old dry-ant pattern doesn't always cut it.

In this particular locale, I want some black ones in various sizes and a big red one, about a size 12, but you don't have to go too far north before you need the one that's cinnamon in back, black in front, with dun wings. Size 14 or 16.

A cricket is a pattern I've never fished, it's just not a popular fly around here, but in the East and Midwest it's almost required equipment. I do fish a beetle—a small, black one—but if I went to Vermont I'd probably want to replace that with a Jassid.

Fly size, as well as pattern, can be a regional matter. Take grasshoppers again. In the West a #12 is considered tiny and a lot of them go up to a #6. But in the East you'll often see hoppers (and crickets, too) starting at #12 and going down as far as a 16 or even 18.

I once heard a brief discussion about this up in Idaho.

"You westerners are not capable of subtlety," said the easterner.

"Oh yeah? Well, you easterners ain't got no big trout," said the cowboy.

Actually, I think smaller hoppers are better than the big bombers for small streams and I now carry them starting at a size 8 or 10 and going down to a 14. I don't know why it makes a difference. When you think about it, it shouldn't. After all, the size of the stream is not what determines the size of the grasshoppers. All I know is, the scale of small streams suggested to me that maybe a small hopper pattern would somehow be more appropriate than a big one. I tried it and it worked. Maybe it's because creek trout are spooky and are frightened by the splat of a size 6 grasshopper hitting the water, or maybe the size 14 is just less intimidating, less of a wrestling match to eat.

When it comes to things like hoppers and crickets, there are infinite variations, but really only two styles: the Whitlock and the Letort—those with legs and those without, respectively. Since I tie most of my own flies, I tend to attempt the fancier patterns in the larger sizes where they're easier to work with. As the flies get smaller, anatomical features begin to disappear, legs among them.

In the grand scheme of things, I don't know how much difference it makes. I like my flies to be as cute and snazzy as possible, but I also like them to tie up fast and be expendable on the water, especially on small streams where snags, trees, and all kinds of things other than trout take them away from you.

When in doubt, it's probably best to tie, or buy, the ones everyone else uses. Maybe they know something you don't, and if not, at least you'll be in style.

Another aspect of regionalism is water type. Many of the small streams I fish are fast rocky freestone creeks with fairly steep gradients along most of their courses and are mostly at altitudes above 5,200 feet. They are cold, somewhat rough, heavily aerated, and devoid of major aquatic vegetation. In other words, they're stonefly water.

In fact, the three stonefly nymph patterns—a big black, a smaller golden, and a #14 yellow—should probably be in the one-box fly selection, they're such common bugs around here. It's things like this that make me reorganize the thing annually. One year the stones are in, the next year they're out. The third year I buy a bigger box.

But let's take a rich, slow-flowing, silt-bottomed creek with luscious beds of aquatic weeds. No stoneflies here, not enough dissolved oxygen and no stones to crawl under anyway. In this stream I'd probably want my wet-fly selection to expand in the direction of scuds, big burrowing mayfly nymphs with marabou gills, and perhaps some sow bugs and backswimmer or water-boat-man beetles.

Warm the same stream up a little bit (but not so much that we're bass fishing) and I'll start thinking in terms of marginal warm-water stuff like damselflies and dragonfly nymphs.

I'll think, but I'll also look, which is usually more educational. I'll get into the water and turn over some rocks to see what's crawling around underneath, look in the weeds to see what's grazing there, maybe even look in the quiet backwaters to see what dead bugs and nymph cases have collected.

Now I'm not much of a trout-stream entomologist, but I do know the adult and nymphal forms of the major insects, recognize the crustaceans, and have a feel for how they all behave. More to the point, I can tell the difference between a little olive one and a big black one.

There's some satisfaction in figuring it out for yourself. You sift through the weeds, find them to be lousy with sow bugs, tie on a sow-bug fly, and catch fish just like an expert. It's even better if you don't have any sow bugs, but the tying kit is back in the truck so you can make some on the spot.

Then again, it's not always that obvious, and a trip to the local fly shop, if there is one, is a good way to back up your own observations with local knowledge and tradition.

Fly tying is an industry now and patterns aren't as deeply regional as they once were. Still, every time I go to a new area and walk into a new fly shop or a gas, worms, and cold beer store, I find at least one fly that's new to me. I ask what the best size is and buy a couple, just in case.

Local Patterns

Local fly patterns fascinate me. An Adams will catch trout just about anywhere, while Uncle Bob's Improved Honey Bug will only work in four streams in the western end of a single county. I'm especially delighted when these flies don't seem to make any sense—that is, don't look like any bug you've ever seen—but there's Uncle Bob himself behind the counter at the gas station saying, "Yup, got ninety-seven trout on that fly just last night."

Bob has been known to exaggerate, but it's not really a weakness. Out-of-town fly fishermen are sometimes hardheaded and suspicious. You have to make things very clear to them.

I'm well aware that fishing writers invent guys like Bob, but that only works because those people actually exist. Many of them have been driven off the larger rivers by the newly introduced scientific fly fishers, but remnant populations of them can still be found wandering the small streams of America where Latin is still a foreign language, where you'll find the trout flies right between the shotgun shells and the light bulbs at the hardware store. If you fish the small streams around there for a while, you'll eventually run into this fellow who says, "Here, try one of these." Regardless of how much you know about trout fishing, try the fly.

Of course, if you fish there long enough you will *become* Uncle Bob, but that's a whole other story.

Water Types

Water type will also have a bearing on the style of fly you'll want to use. For instance, I tend to like the standard English-style dry mayfly patterns with the collar hackle and upright, divided wings because they're

firmly traditional (they look like trout flies are supposed to) and because they work well. But for smoother
water, and especially real spring-creek-style fishing, I
want something like the more sparsely hackled thorax
dry or even the no-hackle. I may stick with the same
three basic colors in the same variety of sizes (unless
there's some hot local pattern you just have to have),
but the style of the flies will change.

Same thing with caddisflies. On smooth water you
might want to replace the Elk Hair Caddis with a crisper
quill-wing pattern like the Henryville or the Hemingway.
In extreme situations you might even want to go to a
sparser, lower-floating fly like the Spring Creek Caddis.

Conversely, if I'm on a rough-and-tumble little tributary to a mountain river, I'll want a high-floating, highly
visible fly that I can see in the rough water. Something
like a Humpy.

Even the action you put on a fly can mean that a
different kind of construction should be used. I've
found that in rough pocket water I can sometimes
move trout that won't go for a nicely dead-drifted dry if I
twitch or even skitter the fly. This is one of those mysterious things that has to do with the collective mood
of the trout.

Okay, fine, but a lightly hackled Adams won't stand
up to that kind of treatment for long—a couple of skit-
ters and suddenly you're fishing a wet fly. I like to have
a few very heavily hackled flies for this, you know, the
ones with a tight palmer hackle *and* a nice, bushy collar—the ones that look like bottle brushes. The one I
use most is just an Adams with a stiff hair tail, palmer
hackle, and oversized wings, size 12 or 14.

That's a fast-water solution to the problem of the
worked fly. In parts of the country where the currents

are glassier you'll find delicate, elegant patterns used for the same thing—flies like the Len Wright Skittering Caddis and the venerable spiders and variants. These are patterns that rely not on volume of hackle to keep the fly up, but on a little bit that is of stunningly high quality. That way the bug can be worked, but it retains its realistic trimness.

Those aren't so much the western and the eastern approaches to a particular fishing tactic as they are ways to deal with worked dry flies in two kinds of water, regardless of where the streams are.

I think a small-stream fly selection should be general in nature because you'll be dealing with creeks and tributaries that are not pounded from dawn to dusk all season by crowds of match-the-hatch-type fishermen. Also, getting very specific is difficult because the detailed hatch charts usually don't exist.

That's not to say the trout in a small stream won't care about fly patterns. I used to think that what we loosely refer to as "selectivity" was trained into a fish population by heavy fly-fishing pressure, especially in places where most of the fish caught were then released to think about what they'd just learned. I still think that happens—it's why you now have to fish a near-perfect #20 Olive Dun Quill to the Blue-Winged Olive hatch on a local catch-and-release area whereas, by all accounts, fifty years ago you could work the same hatch with a #10 Bloody Butcher and, "take your limit in half an hour."

But selectivity also happens naturally, sometimes in surprising places, through a mechanism that is completely beyond me. As far as I'm concerned, it just happens when it feels like it. Here's the most extreme example I know of.

Some years ago a friend and I fished a little creek in the Northwest Territories of Canada that had never been fished by anyone before. We were in a remote fly-in camp where everyone fished the big lake or the big river and paid no attention at all to the surrounding streams and potholes. "Why bother?" they asked.

To make a long story short, we bribed a guide to take us up there, past where the canoe would float, where we happily fished virgin water—the secret dream of every fisherman. This happened to be a grayling stream, and we caught many large fish, but we were amazed to find that they'd eagerly take a #14 Elk Hair Caddis (a fair copy of the bug on the water) but not a #12. And not a #14 Humpy or an Adams, either. And these were only *grayling*, for pete's sake.

In other words, the old "you can catch 'em on anything" myth didn't work there, in the one place I've ever been where it should have—the stream that had never been fished before. We surely would have taken a few fish on something else, but we really nailed them because we had flies that were the right size and the right type, even though they weren't exact copies.

We were delighted, but our guide, who sat on a rock and watched all this, never did quite get it. He kept asking if maybe we shouldn't go back out to the lake and catch some thirty-pound Mackinaws.

If the fly types are geared to the kind of water you're fishing—big and bushy for fast water, sparse and trim for slow—you'll be in business most of the time, although it's worth noting that there are riffles in the slowest water and flat pools now and then appear on the roughest streams. Whatever style of fly I'm fishing, I like to have a few of the other kind, too, and that's where my third fly box came from.

The Comforts of Stuff

Inow own what you'd have to describe as a whole mess of fly rods that were accumulated over the course of about twenty years. They trace two personal histories: first, the search for the perfect all-around rod, then the hunt for various ideal specialty numbers, including *the* small-stream rod. It's been fun, it's been expensive, and it's probably not over.

I tell you this only to show that I have looked into the matter some.

If you walk into almost any fly shop in the country and say you're looking for a small-stream fly rod, they'll probably show you a 7½ foot 4-weight. That's fair, traditional, and hard to argue with. A serviceable 4-weight rod will cast comfortably to the moderate distances needed for small-stream fishing and will deliver standard dry flies, wets, and nymphs (short of Montana-sized weighted stoneflies), although it will be a little wimpy casting all but the smallest streamers.

A rod of that length is light and easy to handle, short enough for tight, well controlled casts, but also long enough to load properly and do most of the actual work of casting, which is why we use rods in the first place.

For roll casting, the longer a rod is the better, but with a 7½-footer you can still roll-cast to short small-stream ranges pretty well. With a rod shorter than 7½ feet, roll casting can become more trouble than it's worth.

Every company that makes fly rods offers at least one 7½ foot 4-weight. It's a standard, a classic, and didn't get that way by accident. On the other hand, there are quite a few other choices on the light end of things.

There are a number of 3-weight rods around now, some 2-weights and, most recently, even a 1-weight. I don't want to toss these off too casually because some good fishermen say they're excellent small-stream rods and seem to like them a lot, and, as we all know, what you like—for reasons that are your own business—is the final gauge of what a good fly rod is.

On the plus side, these dinky little fly rods do deliver flies with incredible delicacy, they're adorable, and if you think the size of the stream you're fishing should determine the size of the rod, they can seem appropriate for the smallest creeks. But they are very, very limited.

For one thing, a 2-weight fly line is for small flies; as one manufacturer says, "fly sizes 14 through 28." In a pinch you can cast something larger, but even with a heavily dressed #10 you'll begin to run into the wind resistance problems that will open your loops and screw up your accuracy, even on short casts. Fishing a lightly weighted nymph or wet fly is a struggle and streamers are out of the question. Essentially, you're limited to small dry flies.

A 2-weight line is also for short casts. That's not a problem on small streams, but these light lines are also for dead-calm days, and that *is* a problem, at least where I come from. I'd rather just go home than try to cast a 2-weight line into the wind.

I'm saying 2-weight *line* instead of *rod* here because

most of the supposed 2-weights I've cast (about a half dozen of them) are, in fact, really 3- or 4-weights. That is, it plainly says "#2 line" on the butt section, but the rod casts better with a heavier line. Depending on the rod, that can be a double-taper 3, weight-forward 4, or even the double-taper 4.

If you already own a 4-weight rod and think you'd like to try a 2, buy the line first and try it on your old rod. You may end up saving yourself several hundred dollars.

For the record, I own a 7½ foot 3-weight and an 8½ foot 2-weight. I fish them both occasionally, but only under absolutely ideal conditions (i.e. the smallest each of streams, fish, and flies, not to mention no wind), and I've never taken either one out without having a real fly rod in the truck as a backup.

I didn't throw small fish in there to be facetious, either. None of the rods I've tried that were light enough to cast a 2-weight line had enough backbone to play a trout of much size with the proper authority. That's not to say you can't land a sixteen- or eighteen-inch trout on a 2-weight rod; you can, but he'll be half dead by the time he makes it to the net. That's fine if you plan to kill and eat him, but when you release a fish after a long fight, his chances of survival get slim. There was a time when extended battles with big trout on light tackle were heroic ("Yes sir, took me forty-five minutes to land him"), but a trout that's going to be released should be played as quickly as possible, and that takes a rod with a little bit of muscle.

"Delicacy" is the big selling point with the ultralight fly rods, but I wonder how much difference there is between a 2-weight and, say, a light-action 5-weight. A fly settles gently on the water if it is cast nicely on whatever rod the fisherman is using at the time. On glassy, smooth water you tie your fly to a long, fine leader, which is all the fish should ever see, and make a long cast or a long drift. If you "line" a trout, it won't matter if you're using a 2- or an 8-weight; he's not going to like it.

You'll also hear that these 2-weights (and, presumably, the 1-weight) will protect very fine tippets. Well, sure, but so will a 4-weight, especially if it's fitted with a smooth reel with the drag set well below "stun" and has a light-handed fisherperson at the controls.

I guess what I'm prepared to say on the subject of light rods is: the lightest "practical" fly rod made is a 4-weight. I mean that in the straightforward sense that if you're spooking trout with the 4-weight, there is almost surely some other answer besides running down to the fly shop and buying a 2-weight. A longer leader, finer tippet, longer drift, better stalk, or maybe trying again tomorrow.

Either that or there's no answer at all, which is always a possibility.

I should also say that if you want to fish a very light rod because it's fun, go ahead and do so with my blessing. Fun—or "satisfaction," if you prefer the more high-sounding word—is the bottom line. And, as I said, I do fish my own 2- and 3-weight rods sometimes, although I've now come to think of them as light action 4s. They're great when you need a photograph of a guy with his rod bent double on a trout, but the fish in the creek are only six inches long. Still, a good small-stream rod should be light enough to let the fish show off, but heavy enough to *handle* those same fish, and an extremely light rod often just can't keep that balance.

The 5-Weight Rod

I have a couple of standard 4-weights that I use often enough, two 7½-footers and an 8½-footer, but more and more of my small-stream fishing is done with a 5-weight, which, when fished with a long leader and a light touch, has all the delicacy of a 4, plus a little more punch for streamers and wind. In other words, it's more versatile, which is an advantage I like. A light little dry-fly rod is fine except on those days when you have to go about things a little differently. And I've never been able to predict when those days will come along.

The 5-weight is what I currently feel most comfortable with, but I'll admit that the difference between a 4- and a 5-weight rod (or a 5 and a 6 for that matter) is negligible.

Rod Length and Line Weight

Rod length is also an important consideration, maybe even more important than line weight in some situations, and this is where the character of the actual stream in question will make a big difference.

The shortest fly rod I have is a 6½ foot 5-weight that I reserve for the tightest, brushiest creeks. It's a sweet little rod and one of the few I've seen that is that short but still casts well. I consider it to be a very specialized rod, but A. K., who lived for years in Michigan, told me that if I fished some of the places he used to I'd have worn the thing out by now, or have tangled it up in the alders and broken it.

As I said, a 7½ foot rod—not to mention the occasional 7 foot-9 incher—is a good small-stream compromise with some of the advantages of both shorter and longer rods. There are a lot of fine ones around.

On the other end of the scale, there are times when

A pair of light 5-weight bamboo rods: possibly the ideal small-stream rod.

a nice long rod, say nine or even ten feet, is the best choice. I'm thinking primarily of meadow streams where there are few casting impediments and also not much cover: places where you need reach and good line control. Long rods are also useful for dapping and especially nymphing where, again, reach is important, and they're sublime for roll casting. Paradoxically, the best rod for a very small stream with lots of ticklish casting problems might just be a long one. If you want a historical precedent for that, consider the old-time "dapping" rods, those long, willowy things that would let you fish the whole stream without casting.

I guess at this point we're back to a matter of style again. If you're fishing a small creek and are one of those who likes to actually fly cast, you'll probably want a pretty short rod, one that will let you throw those low, tight loops. If you do a lot of dapping and roll casting or you're a serious nymph fisher, you'll probably prefer something considerably longer for the same stream. I'm not prepared to say which way you'll catch more trout or have a better time. I've done it both ways and I'd have to call it a tie.

And there are the inevitable regional variations. I once met a guide in Montana who did all his small-stream fishing with a 7½ foot 7-weight loaded with a weight-forward 8 line because the fish were big and the wind was strong. He looked at my 4-weight as if to say "Jeeze, another tourist," and asked, "Did you bring a heavier rod with ya?" This was on a stream that was roughly as wide as it was deep—about ten feet in both directions—that had just that year yielded a twelve-pound brown trout: a fish that one might have to put some wood to, as they say. That short 7/8 rod of his is not what most of us would think of as a small-stream tool, but it was ideal for wrestling with big browns in tight cover.

Casting Ranges

I once worked in a fly shop and the hardest thing I had to do there was help customers pick out fly rods— customers who didn't already know exactly what they wanted, that is. What most chose to do was take every rod in the store out into the parking lot for a test drive and then buy the one they could cast the farthest with. I spent a lot of time talking them down, saying things like, "Well, that's very nice, but most of the casts you'll be making around here will be more like from here to that pickup truck, less than thirty feet—sometimes considerably less."

I think the point is, a good small-stream rod should be of a comfortable length for your style and the streams in question and it should cast well at the short ranges you'll be fishing. The action of the rod has a lot to do with that. Of course, you'll decide for yourself what kind of fly rod you like best, but I think that in the hands of an average caster, a slow-action rod will cast better in close than a fast, or "dry fly" action. A rod's action is determined largely by its taper, but the line you put on it can also make a big difference.

I've always preferred double-taper fly lines because they cast nicely at moderate ranges and can be turned around when you wear out one end, giving you what amounts to two lines for the price of one. For what a good fly line costs these days, that's not unimportant. But on most small streams you're looking at casts in the short-range to point-blank category and for that you want to get more weight out past the rod tip sooner.

One way to do that is to make the half step up to a weight-forward line, that is, put a WF-5 on your 4-weight, or whatever. The fatter, shorter taper loads the rod with less line out and gives it better (that is, slower) action on shorter casts. Of course, weight-forwards can't be turned around, so, given the same amount of fishing, you'll buy twice as many of them as you would double-tapers.

It's an old habit of mine to worry about things like that, but, in the end, the tackle industry usually wins. I'm indulgent when it comes to my fly rods; if one of them really wants the more expensive line, then that's what it gets.

Another option is to go to the next size double-taper line, say a DT-6 on your 5-weight rod. This has worked fine on most of the rods I've tried it with, but be advised that this is for very short casts in tight places. Out at even normal casting ranges, let alone long casts, you are overloading the rod. At best it might not cast very well, at worst you could damage it.

It all depends on the individual rod. If you have a slow-action rod that's for, say, a double-taper 5 line, going up to a weight-forward or double-taper 6 might slow it down too much. If you have an old, very limber, noodly rod with what they used to call a wet-fly action, you might want to step *down* a line size, even for short casts. Every rod you pick up will be a little different, with its own peculiar charms and eccentricities. Each one should be treated as an individual, not as a generic X-weight.

By the way, if a rod says it's for, say, a 5 line, that usually refers to the double-taper. If it says "5 or 6" it means DT-5 or weight-forward 6. Except for Orvis. Orvis is the only rod company I know of that rates their rods for the weight-forward line. If it's a 5-weight Orvis, it uses a weight-forward 5, which, to the rest of the world, makes it a 4-weight.

I mention that only because I've seen it cause some confusion. The best thing to do is try a few different lines on any rod to see which one works the best for you. I have a couple of rods that I fish with as many as three different line weights depending on the conditions, the lines getting heavier as the casting distances get shorter.

And for small-stream fishing we're talking about floating lines. Sink-tips and full sinkers are useful so seldom I hardly ever carry one unless there's a lake at the upper end of the creek and I plan to fish that, too.

I guess if I had to have a single small-stream fly rod, it would be a 7½ foot 4-weight that had a graceful, but still slightly tippy, action with a weight-forward 5 line. I have two like that, one a little slower than the other.

But then for very demanding smooth-water conditions in tight quarters, I'll sometimes take the 7½ foot 3-weight loaded with a weight-forward 4 line. This one is poor in the wind and not gutsy enough for larger flies, but as a small dry-fly rod it's lovely, and some mornings you just wake up and say "the hell with nymphs, streamers, versatility, and practicality. Today I'm gonna catch 'em on dry flies or I'm not gonna catch 'em at all."

In the same kind of spot, but with a little more room to cast, I might rather take the 8½ foot 4-weight and a spare spool. With the double-taper 4 this is a quick dry-fly rod with a tip fast enough to make it excellent for nymphing. With the weight-forward 5 it will handle a little wind and throw a small streamer comfortably.

A little more wind and/or bigger fish and I'll want

either the 8 foot or the 8½ foot 5-weight so maybe I can land the big ones in less than half an hour.

And so it goes. The fact is, I like fly rods. As expensive habits go, it's harmless and more socially acceptable than some.

Bamboo Rods

I don't know if I should even bother discussing rod materials here because almost everyone uses graphite now and likes it. Still, let me put in a word for split-bamboo rods. Pricey? They can be, yes. Classy? You bet. But a good medium-action bamboo could just be the ultimate small-stream fly rod.

The stiff butt gives you all kinds of stubborn leverage for playing fish while the pliant wood tip goes easy on tippets, and those two elements fit together into an indescribable feel that you can really get used to.

Same thing with casting. Bamboo doesn't have the power you're always hearing about in connection with graphite, but I think that's overrated in fly rods. Raw power isn't what you need for small-stream fishing; what you need is a graceful, fluid, forgiving, slow-line-speed action that will help you make delicate, accurate, close-range casts. I've fished a lot of graphites and have been perfectly happy with most of them, but I've yet to see one that was as satisfying and (let's admit it) down-right easy to cast as a quality light-line bamboo rod. In the shorter lengths, even the extra added weight of the wood rod feels good. It seems to load all by itself. All you have to do is point it where you want the line to go.

And while we're admitting things, bamboo rods *are* awfully snazzy. They fairly reek of old-timey British tra-dition and, even though anyone will tell you I'm not a high-tone fisherman, I still can't help being a sucker for that sort of thing: a small, quiet stream, a mayfly hatch, a wheat-colored bamboo rod with a little English reel on it . . . this is a powerful mystique and it explains why some fishermen are more polite on the stream than they are at home.

If I ever felt the need to justify the money I've spent on bamboo fly rods, I'd probably have a hard time doing it. Luckily, it's never come up. Still, the fly rod is one of the few pieces of fishing gear that isn't expendable, the one that can, and often does, outlive even the fisherman. It's one of those areas of life where quality pays off.

Leaders

On small streams I like to fish a leader that's roughly the same length as the rod I'm using, which makes most of mine about 7½ or 8 feet. A short leader is easier for me to control and in the tight quarters of most small streams I don't feel that I need anything longer to cover my cast. I've also found that if the leader is about as long as the rod, I have a sort of instinctive feel for it and can gauge ranges more closely to get better accuracy. That may be a personal quirk, but it works.

Okay, I do often tie on a longer tippet when dry-fly fishing in slow currents or where the trout are especially spooky, and sometimes this will make a noticeable difference. It's just more fiddling around, which is something you can't let bother you if you're going to fly fish. It's part of the sport. On the other hand, when a trout refuses to take your fly, the answer isn't always to step down from a 5X tippet to a 6X, and then from a 6 to a 7. I always try to figure out how I can make my drift better before I start to re-rig. Many times the problem turns out to be operator error rather than tippet size.

In other words, it's a poor workman who blames his tools before he's eliminated all the other more likely possibilities.

Speaking of fiddling around, I'm one of those cranks who tie their own leaders. Don't worry, I'm not going to get into the intricacies of leader design, but I'll take a minute to tell you all I know about it. I think the best leaders are the ones with a gradual taper at the fat end, a short, fast taper just past the middle, and a long tippet. The butt section should be of stiff monofilament to hold the energy of the cast as it comes down the line, and the forward section, where you need finesse for good drifts, should be of a limper material. A well-designed leader is especially important on small streams where the casts are sometimes so short you'll have more leader than line out past the tip top guide. In fact, you should be able to cast a good leader all by itself.

End of treatise.

I automatically tie most of my leaders ending with a 4X wear section, to which I generally tie a 5X tippet when I go fishing. 5X seems to work best for me on small streams because it's fine enough for delicate casts and good dead drifts, but still pretty strong. Naturally I'll go lighter when I feel I have to, but I want to fish the strongest tippet that will still do the job.

My leaders are tied directly to their fly lines and whatever adjustments I make to the terminal ends involve cutting back and/or retying sections of mono. It's not as laborious as it sounds, although cold fingers can slow things down some. I know a few fly fishers who have a leader butt with a perfection loop in it tied to the end of their line and who carry a wallet filled with leaders, also with loops, any one of which can be put on in a matter of seconds. That's a time-honored way to do it, but I guess I've just never felt the need for all those different leaders. The only time it would be handy would be for changing from a long, fine dry-fly leader to a shorter, stouter nymph leader for deep pools, although I've found that in practice a fairly short dry-fly leader works just fine for nymphing.

There are a lot of leader "systems" on the market now with braided butt sections; those, and the 2-weight rods, are the hot new items this year. I may be missing something here, but it seems to me the braided section is nothing more than an extension of the fly line's forward taper, which is exactly what the fat end of a conventional leader is. It strikes me as something you just don't need. I mean, the end of your fly line is already there, why add another three feet to it?

Then again, maybe I'm just being tight. I'll happily spend hundreds of dollars on a fly rod, but a couple of extra bucks for a braided leader butt just rubs me the wrong way. And anyway, I have developed a studied resistance to "the hot new item this year." Talk to me again in a couple of seasons.

Boots

As I said, I do my small-stream fishing in hip boots (if I can't get around in hippers, I'm not on a small stream) and I wish I could decide whether or not it's worth buying the good expensive ones. I've gone both ways, paying as little as twelve dollars and as much as eighty-some, and have never had a pair last through two seasons without having to be patched. The leaks appear on the knees and the toes (from crawling), and on the insides of the legs where they rub together while

I'm walking. That's not counting barbed-wire nicks, which can be anywhere.

I'm as hard on hippers as kids are on jeans, something I take a certain amount of pride in. As a friend once said, "You know you've lost it when your pants wear out in the ass before the knees go."

Actually, I don't own a pair of hip boots at the moment. The last pair went in the trash in the fall, after I'd spent several weeks searching for the mystery leak. It was somewhere in the right foot, presumably in the few square inches that weren't already slathered with Barge Cement. But then the rest of them was already covered with patches and was starting to look like a clown suit. I could see it was a losing battle. Very soon now I'll have to start shopping for a new pair.

I have some minor brand loyalties in operation, but I've never gotten attached to an actual pair of waders of any kind. By the time I finally lose patience and pitch them, the last thing I feel is sentiment. They let me down. I mean, they let me get *wet*. If they lasted a decent amount of time, I might buy another pair just like them, but that's as close as I'll ever come to having warm feelings for waders.

I wish I could say that every time I buy a new pair, the first thing I do is glue knee patches on them. I should do that, knowing that in half a summer's creek fishing I'll have chewed little pinhole leaks there from kneeling in the gravel, but I just don't ever seem to get around to it. Something perverse in me makes me wait until cold stream water is trickling down my leg and pooling in the boot.

I met a man once who wore those roofer's kneepads over his hippers. They stopped leaks from developing, he said, but mostly they saved wear and tear on his own knees. It struck me as a good idea. Have you ever knelt down wrong on a little pointed rock and electrified the nerves in that whole side of your body? A big, beautiful trout is rising not twenty feet away and you're hobbling around going, "Ow, ow, ow."

The next pair of hippers will probably be of the fairly expensive variety, as opposed to "ditch boots," because the good ones come with felt soles, which I think is a must for wading any rocky-bottomed stream. Wading safety on small streams is seldom talked about, but falls can be nasty. I've glued felts to rubber-soled hippers, but I've never had them stay on for very long.

I also plan to get the kind that are all smooth rubber, rather than the ones with canvas uppers. It's too hard to find leaks in canvas.

Neoprene waders have gotten very popular recently and lately I've seen some neoprene hip boots. I like the neoprene chest waders just fine. They're a bit of a struggle to get into, but once you're in they're warm and comfortable. The only problem I have is that they're pretty easy to poke holes in, so if you try the hippers, be a little careful with them, especially around barbed wire and the sharp sticks in beaver dams.

Maybe the best thing to do is get a good patch kit and learn to live with the fact that your hip boots will sooner or later leak—probably in the coldest water and as far from a pair of dry socks as you've gotten all year. As someone once said, leaky waders are one of the three things in life you can count on, the other two being death and taxes.

Odds and Ends

My favorite small streams are the ones that require a little bit of walking to get into, consequently my creek-fishing program is geared largely for lightness and mobility. I try to keep the gear down to two or three fly boxes, the usual handful of odds and ends (clippers, leader spools, etc.), sandwich, dry matches, and rain gear. For short jaunts in warm weather, I can get all that in the vest, and on cooler days I can also stash a sweater in the back pouch.

For trips that will stretch into a full day, I'll usually wear a medium-sized day pack. Basically, this allows for the coffee pot, which, in turn, sets the stage for the leisurely coffee *break*.

I know a few fishermen who are horrified at the idea of tossing together a little twig fire, brewing up a pot, and kicking back for half an hour to relax, look at the trees, and listen to the birdies sing. They came to fish, by God, and that's what they're gonna do—the poor bastards.

About half the fly fishermen I know strap on a small pack for creek trips. Some of them fill said pack with fishing tackle—more fly boxes, spare spools, insect nets, and so on. Others bring the coffee pot, more lunch, flask of brandy, and other things geared more to personal comfort than to fishing success. Still others get a larger pack and bring all that stuff and more. A pack is one of the handiest things ever invented, but, like a fly vest with too many pockets, it can sucker you into bringing along all kinds of things you'll never use.

Stuff in general, whether it's fishing tackle or survival gear, can be tremendously comforting. "I am ready" you think as you grunt into the straps of the fifty-pound backpack. But then that comfort turns on you and by noon you're thinking, "I am ready to be airlifted out of here."

The problem is magnified on longer hikes, the ones

where you'll be sleeping out there for a night or more. You want to go as lightly as possible, but every piece of camping gear eliminates some fishing tackle, and vice versa. If the pack is too heavy you won't be able to cover much ground and you'll beat yourself up too much. If you go too light you can end up nice and mobile, but also cold, wet, and hungry.

Since I'm basically a softy, I tend to look to the essentials of personal comfort first: good sleeping bag, insulated ground cloth, proper clothing, and good rain gear. I've never used a tent, even one of those little backpacking numbers, that wasn't too heavy to carry, so I go in the Boy Scout style with a shelter half and some nylon cord that can be fashioned into a rain fly or lean-to arrangement. This works fine for the occasional shower, but I'll admit it can come up short in a genuine storm.

My food is mostly of the "just add water" variety, sometimes backed up with a treat, like a can of Dinty Moore beef stew. Kitchen utensils consist of frying pan, coffee pot, tin cup, fork, spoon, and pocketknife.

I've carried hip boots to change into, fished without hip boots, and hiked *in* the hip boots at various times and have yet to find the solution to that particular problem, although backpacking might be the place where the neoprene hippers would really come in handy. All I'll say is, if you're going to hike in the hip boots, make sure they fit well.

That's what I figure I need to stay out for a few nights, or even just a single night, for that matter. It's already a good load to have to carry on your back and we don't even have the fishing tackle in there yet.

In fact, if you're like me and spend half of every season groaning under an enormous fly vest, you should do some backpacking just to see how little you really need. A handful of odds and ends in one shirt pocket, rod and reel, of course, and somewhere between one and three fly boxes, depending on how well you know the water or how cocky you feel. The vest stays at home; it's just extra weight.

It's not much, considering that it's the focus of the entire expedition. All together it shouldn't weigh much more than that big can of stew.

Where There are Trout, There's Hope

Time does march on and it's possible to lose track of places. A week ago, I went back to a spot I hadn't fished in a good eight years or more because I suddenly couldn't remember why I hadn't been there in so long. It had always been good, by which I mean I had sometimes caught trout and sometimes not, but they had always been there—brook trout, in this case.

I guess it's just the down side to wanderlust; different places are tantalizing, but new discoveries can cause you to neglect old discoveries.

The place was a lake—a reservoir, actually. It was an old impoundment from the mining and narrow-gauge railroad days that had backed up a largely insignificant little mountain stream with a primitive earthen dam, which, over the years, had softened and gone wild to the point where you had to go out of your way to notice that it wasn't a glacial esker or something.

The lake was pretty and people fished it, since it was at the end of something of a road. But the stream above the lake, flowing out of a partially wooded gulch several miles wide, was not hit much except for its inlet, where the trout would collect in the evenings. There were some good brookies up there, both in some wide bends not far above the lake and farther up in a string of beaver ponds.

It was as if this creek had been laid out to discourage

the marginally curious. The inevitable fisherman's trail went up the bank for a few hundred yards along a stretch of stream that was shallow, fast, and largely troutless, and stopped just out of sight of the first good water. You could see the exact spot where the lake fishermen had wandered up and said, "Well, nothing much up here," and then headed back to catch the evening rise at the inlet.

The trout in the creek seldom went past ten inches. In fact, a ten-inch brookie there would make your day, but they were wild and handsome—as was the countryside—and, as far as I could ever tell, precious few people knew they were there. It had been a place to camp, fish, fry and eat the occasional fresh brook trout, and either remember or forget, depending on how the previous days had been going.

You students of irony will appreciate the fact that when I took my friend Mike Price there last week the lake was gone. Where the old dike had once been there was now a lonesome fence post holding a sign. The sign—somewhat weathered and hard to read—said the dam had been taken out because it was unsafe. There was a faded phone number you could call for "further information," and I was on the way back to the truck for a pen and notebook to write it down when I realized I didn't *need* any further information.

As it turned out, the missing lake was only part of the story. The bend pools had silted in badly because the abandoned beaver ponds above them had first silted in themselves and then blown out in the high flows of one of the spring runoffs since I'd been there last. In short, the place had reverted back to what it had been in the days before the little reservoir: a pretty little mountain creek that had probably never held trout because it was too small, too high, and too rugged.

It was late October—the day before Halloween, in fact—and the brookies would have been moving out of the lake to spawn in the stream. This used to be when the biggest trout were in evidence, when you could hope to crack ten inches or maybe even a foot.

It had begun to snow. We traded the fly rods for shotguns then and went looking for grouse. I flushed one and missed.

And then we were cold and wet and beginning to worry about the condition of the road we had to get out on. Every year people get caught out in the bushes in these early snows and have to be rescued, which can be both dangerous and embarrassing. So we left. We decided the trip was complete when we stopped at a bar on the way home, a cozy little roadhouse where we figured to sit by the fireplace and watch the snow fall for a while, only to find that it had been closed.

These things happen to fishermen and they're even enjoyable in a way, often making for better stories than success. Of course, you don't like to have too many like that in a row.

There's even a standard procedure. First, you feel sorry for yourself. You've paid your dues, you think, and you deserve better than this. Then it occurs to you that dues have to be paid regularly—often in advance—and that's probably what this was. A large part of finding out where the fish are is finding out where they *aren't*.

Then, perhaps, back at home with the gear stored, you begin to cogitate. The beaver ponds got old and died, but where are the beavers? Well, maybe they were trapped off, though that's doubtful. Maybe when things went to hell they died off. That happens. Then again, maybe they moved downstream.

Between where the lake used to be and the main dirt road there are several miles of stream. I never went that way because I liked the stretch above the lake so much. Who knows what's down there? Not me. I never even noticed a trail.

In fact, you know that when they take out these old, rotten dams that are so dangerous—whether they use dynamite or heavy equipment—they drain them first, and with the water go the trout. If there's anything like good habitat down below, it could be lousy with brook trout, and all but the smartest fishermen who used to go there did exactly what you just did: they wrote it off and went home.

Literally or figuratively, you slap yourself on the forehead and say, "WE WENT THE WRONG WAY!"

And that phone number you didn't bother to take down . . . Now you realize what further information you could use. When did they drain the reservoir and blow the dam? Eight years ago or last season? If too much time has passed it might not matter, but if it was last season, or maybe the season before, all the fish that used to be in the lake could be down there in the beaver ponds and plunge pools downstream.

You picture the fading sign on the fence post up there with snow falling around it (faded, yes, but a sign can fade in a single year of sun and wind) and it occurs to you that you may not be as smart as you thought you were.

You might not be able to get in there again until spring, but that's okay. A dangerous antique back-country reservoir would be the business of the Corps of Engineers, or, if not, then they'd know whose business it is. Whoever, they're in the book. Two or three phone calls come Monday morning and you'll know.

I guess the point is, where there are trout, there's hope.

In most trout-fishing areas it's the larger rivers that are the best known and the most crowded with fishermen, a majority of the fishermen, in fact, all standing in a fraction of the miles of flowing water in that corner of the state. And why not? That's usually where the biggest trout are caught and it's also where you can just about set your watch by the regular, predictable hatches. It's a known commodity, a place where you can actually plan a trip in such confident terms as "going to The Henry's Fork in June for the green drake hatch."

I'd even go so far as to say that a healthy population of big trout is just one of the elements that makes a famous river famous. The other is predictability.

Unpredictability

Most of the small streams aren't like that. They don't usually have enough big trout to draw a crowd, nor is there a chart somewhere to tell you such-and-such of a hatch will be on in the first three weeks of August when you can catch them on this pattern right here—at $1.50 per fly at the shop right on the river. You can be on your own fishing a small stream, faced with figuring the whole thing out for yourself.

In the end, you'll have to string up a rod and go find out, which is the part I like best, but it doesn't hurt to do a little research first. In some cases you'll have to actually locate the streams before you do anything else. They don't all flow right next to the road.

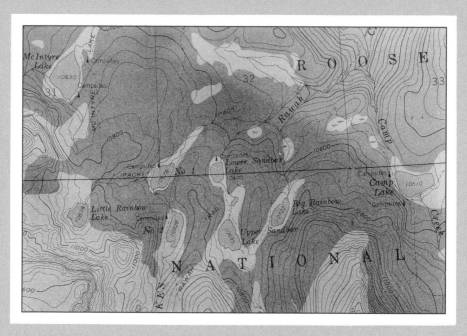

Trace headwater streams on a good map.

Scouting

It's naturally best to do your small-stream scouting in good trout country, some place where there are miles and miles of creeks feeding several good rivers. Any river drainage with trout in it will do, regardless of where it happens to be. For instance, where I'm sitting right now is a two-hour drive from the closest place in the state that is known for its hot trout fishing, but I could fish the small streams in two counties around here all season and never run out of places to go. For that matter, I've been doing just that for the better part of two decades and the major debate is still between places I haven't fished yet and spots I want to get back to. There are lots of areas like this around the country— more than most of us think. You don't have to live in West Yellowstone, Montana, although that wouldn't hurt, either.

Maps

The best place to start is with a map—or maybe I should say *maps*. The fishing maps published by various state divisions of fish and game are usually a good place to begin because they show the rivers in some detail and leave off all the superfluous and unimportant details other maps insist on including, like towns and things. These maps cover entire states as a rule, so they're not too tightly focused, but all but the smallest creeks will at least be hinted at.

For a closer view, get the appropriate county map or, better yet, the one covering the public land in the area. These will be the official ones put out by state and national forests, parks, and such. They'll be pretty good in terms of showing you exactly what creeks are there, what kind of access there is and the general type of country they're in.

For areas where fishing is a big deal, there may be specific fisherman's maps that are published through fly shops and/or local sportsmen's groups. I have a stack of these showing several famous trout rivers in my part of the country. They're all useful, but many of them have the same failing.

Oh, they cover the Big River just fine, showing the actual shape and size of the stretch of it in question, sometimes the names of the more well-known pools, and sometimes even a brief hatch chart, but they seldom go into much detail on the feeder creeks. Tributaries are shown where they enter the river, but upstream they just peter off into aimless blue lines sketched by cartographers who believed them to be unimportant.

Your most detailed and revealing shot at a given small area will be one of the topographic maps available from the U.S. Geological Survey. These are typically the best maps available, although they still show the smaller streams as nothing more than blue lines.

Of course, the best maps by far are the ones drawn hastily by other fishermen on the backs of paper napkins.

I love maps; love to get the boys together on a slow winter afternoon and pour over them, find places— sometimes right up the road—where none of us have ever been.

"You ever get up in here?"

"No. You?"

And that faraway look goes around the table from fisherman to fisherman. Never having seen a stretch of trout stream is reason enough to go. You know the feeling. Maybe the biggest trout in the whole creek is in that one stretch you haven't fished yet.

Around home you can just take a day, stuff the coffee pot and a couple of sandwiches in a day pack, and go check it out. If the fish are small, well, that happens, right? If nothing else, you had a nice walk.

Further Research and Deeper Thinking

On the other hand, maybe you prefer to, as they say now, "optimize" your chances by further research or some deeper thinking on the matter.

Is the mystery stretch of water on a creek that is known as a pretty good trout stream and this is just a piece of it that's a little harder to get to? Go. Good trout streams don't just go to hell for no reason. If there are fish downstream where everyone fishes it, there are probably trout upstream, too.

It's so hard to get to that it's known locally as Cardiac Canyon? Work out for two weeks and *then* go. I hate to admit this, but fishermen (yes, even fly fishermen) are basically lazy. They want huge trout, and lots of them, within sight of the car. The tougher the access to a stretch of stream, the less it's fished, and the less it's fished, the better the fishing will be, all things being equal.

Is access a problem because the place is fenced or posted? The smartest fishermen I know—the guys I really admire—are the ones who are skeptical of things like that. If the truth was known, a lot of public land in this country is posted illegally. Much of it is Bureau of Land Management land that's leased to ranchers who put "No Trespassing" signs up, either because they think they have a right to or because they know they can usually get away with it. In some cases local land-owners will post Forest Service land or close public access roads. In some parts of the country this is a local tradition.

Now let me be as clear as I can be on this. Most "Keep Out" signs are legal and should be respected, but if you have doubts, it can't hurt to do some checking. The BLM, Forest Service, and other agencies typically don't have the manpower to police these things themselves, but they'll usually run it down for you if you're persistent, and they will act on violations when brought to their attention by a citizen.

Things like this can take some doing, but if you pull one off you'll be a local hero—although, if you're smart, you *won't* be a hero because you won't tell anyone about it. You'll just quietly fish there.

Okay, maybe it really is private, but it still looks awfully good in there behind the fence. There's no law against asking for permission to fish. Success or failure comes on a case-by-case basis here, although there are some regional tendencies. If I had to make a broad statement, I'd say that in heavily populated parts of the country, private means private, while in more open country people are a bit less uptight about these things. But don't hold me to that.

There's an art to asking for permission to fish, but no secret. Just be polite, patient, and prepared to take no for an answer. To put it another way, don't lose sight of the fact that you're asking a total stranger for a big favor.

If you do manage to get on a private stream, offer to share your catch, or release all your fish, or whatever; close gates behind you; don't climb barbed wire fences; don't litter; stop and say thanks on the way out and otherwise act like a gentleman. If you're not a gentleman, fake it. It's not hard to do for short periods of time.

It goes without saying that if a stream is posted by a private fishing club, it's a waste of time even to ask.

Something else you'll want to try to figure out is if there are any fish in the stream and, if so, are there enough good-sized ones to make fishing it worthwhile. Given the time, I'll fish anywhere under just about any circumstances. I consider the mere act of fly fishing worth doing for its own sake. I do, however, require some fish, and I like for at least a few of them to be what we'll call—for lack of a better term—keeper-sized. You know, trout you wouldn't be ashamed of if you decided to bring a few home.

The Word on the Stream

Well, what's The Word on the stream? The Word is out there somewhere—I doubt there's a single small stream in the United States that isn't known well by some fisherman—but it can range from common knowledge to whispered speculation.

The St. Vrain drainage here is a good example. The places that are easily accessible are widely known to be decent little trout streams where you can catch browns and some rainbows. At any point where you can see the stream from the car window, it's not unusual to also see a fly fisher, and it's entirely possible that he was told about the spot by someone at a local sporting goods store or fly shop.

In the places where the main forks wander away from the roads, sometimes through some rugged country, there is less common knowledge about them floating around for free, fewer fishermen, and sometimes some better than average fishing.

The same is true where they disappear upstream into the roadless wilderness area and, at one point, the national park. Somewhere in there the brook trout and cutthroats begin to show up, but even those of us who have fished the area for a long time would be hard pressed to tell you exactly where that happens.

Information on the more remote stretches is harder to get, that is, more difficult to first find the people who know, and then to get it out of them.

At some point in here, you get into some downright obscure areas. There's one little creek—depending on where you start downstream, it's a fourth- or fifth-order tributary—that no one seems to know about except one old guy who used to fish it back when the daily limit was twenty-five trout. He said one summer he "took a couple limits of cutthroats" there.

Judging by the size of the thing where it empties into the next creek, where I've passed it a couple of times, two limits of twenty-five trout is about all it could hold and the guy probably very nearly fished it out during that summer in the 1930s. But that was a long time ago.

I never paid much attention to it before that conversation, and I have yet to actually go and fish it, but I did look at it on the map. There are, of course, miles of it up there, most of it a long way from any road, and I know for a fact that there were at least fifty trout in it fifty-some years ago.

Evaluating Stories and Rumors

For the serious small-stream fly fisher, evaluating stories and rumors is as important a skill as casting.

The fact is, the truth is seldom told about trout streams. In the reports you get, from whatever source, they're made to sound either better or worse than they really are. And, yes, fishermen do lie from time to time. As you ask around about an area, be suspicious of stories about too many trout that were all too big, and when someone tells you—perhaps a little too quickly— that he's never fished there or it's no good, watch his eyes.

There are other good sources of information about small streams besides fellow fishermen. I like to think of typical small-stream country as wild and lonely. Much of it is for the most part, but in some areas trout have been planted or "reintroduced," habitat improvement projects have been undertaken, and population, growth rate, and even aquatic-insect studies have been done. And the people who do that like to follow up with studies. Much of this sort of thing centers on lakes and rivers, but also has a bearing on the small streams in the area.

A case in point: Some years ago an exotic strain of rainbow-cutthroat hybrid trout were introduced into a mountain lake near here. It was a big deal with lots of fanfare and it was followed closely by local fishermen, including this one. A few years later, in the course of doing a follow-up story for the local newspaper, I was talking to the biologist in charge of the project. Out of idle curiosity I asked him why the special regulations extended up and down the streams that fed and drained the lake. "I didn't think you'd stocked the streams," I said.

"We didn't," the guy answered, "but we know that these fish will eventually work their way out into the streams and establish resident populations."

Suddenly, through dumb luck and some basic in-quisitiveness, I knew something that everyone else didn't know. Sure, I should have figured it out for my-self, as others surely have, but never mind about that. I know it now. To this day, the lake can get crowded, but it's rare to see someone fishing the stream.

Needless to say, none of this went into the newspaper story.

State fisheries biologists often know a lot about the small streams; the information is accurate and they're usually pretty free with it. It's best to have a couple of specific places to ask about and keep in mind that this will probably take a number of phone calls. With most of the divisions of wildlife I've dealt with, you first have to get past the receptionist and the recorded fishing-information message that tells you which reservoirs have recently been stocked, then find out who knows about the area you're interested in, and then actually get in touch with that person. It can take a while, espe-cially since the guy you really want to talk to is invari-ably "in the field" and won't be back in the office until, "Oh, I don't know, maybe next week sometime."

I don't hold that against anyone, by the way. In fact, it has a nice ring to it. Yup, that's the guy I want, the one who is currently "in the field," calling those trout by their first names.

Local guide services are also good sources of infor-mation, especially for areas you're not familiar with. You can find out about them through state guides' associations, local chambers of commerce, or some-times the department of fish and game. Once again, you're looking at more than one phone call.

Ask about walking or horse pack trips to small streams, along with particulars like the names of the streams and distances traveled. Some guides are into this sort of thing in a big way, while others only want to float you down the big river for the big bucks. If possible, talk to more than one in the area.

You can use a guide service as a starting point for your own research. Get the names of a couple of streams from them, then check with the fish and wildlife guys about the fishing, the forest service about the access, USGS about the maps, and so on.

Or you can think seriously about hiring the guide. One of the great, seldom talked about values of a good guide is that he can get you to those out-of-the-way little creeks that it would take you a month of hiking to locate on your own. A guide who knows about these places, likes them, and who is otherwise competent is probably going to be worth the money.

You may have to come to an understanding with the guide here. He's likely to assume, based on prior experience with sports, that what you really want is lots of twenty-inch trout, regardless of what you tell him. You have to make him understand that you actually want to fish a small stream and, although you naturally want the biggest fish possible, you don't expect miracles.

While you're at it, get that straight in your own head, too. You want peace, quiet, wildlife, scenery, wild trout, and you *don't* expect miracles. What I like to do is give myself a couple of days to fish the big river to get that out of my system, and then go wandering around on some small stream after I've calmed down a little.

There's a third possibility. This is where the guide says, "Look, I don't do trips like that, but if you really want a nice little stream, try such-and-such creek four miles upstream from the campground. And take some #14 olive caddisflies."

This is not something you can count on or realistically expect, but it does happen. Sometimes we small-stream types just don't interface properly with the business end of fly fishing; they don't quite know what to do with us and so they toss us what we really want for no charge—just get off the phone so I can book another float trip.

Most of the time you will not get the entire story on a small stream just by doing research. What you'll end up with is some tantalizing, but incomplete, information. This is where you'll have to do a little thinking.

Is the creek in question a tributary to a "good" trout stream? That's an excellent sign. Given half a chance, trout will spread.

Does it feed a lake or reservoir? If so, what's in there, brown trout or carp? You may not be able to find anyone who knows much about the stream, but somebody surely knows about the lake. Whatever lives in the lake will probably run up the stream, if not permanently, then at least on a seasonal basis.

If the stream is in the backcountry, does it flow out of a headwater lake or, better yet, does it connect some lakes? The creeks in the vicinity of trout lakes can be real sleepers. When you're talking to various agency people about the fish in a given stream, remember to ask about the lakes in the area, and study the map so you know which streams connect with which lakes.

Typically, the farther upstream you go on a river system, the smaller the creeks—and the trout—will be. In theory, the best creek is the immediate tributary to the river. The tributaries to *that* stream will be a bit smaller, with less water and all-around lower quality habitat, and so on until you reach the tiny springs and snow-melt trickles where even a little fish would have trouble staying wet. But that's on a textbook drainage. In practice, the small streams will be periodically supercharged by lakes and reservoirs and also by pockets of unusually good habitat.

I know of several that are marginal as trout habitat lower down on their drainages—where people see them and write them off—but that spread out into some very sweet stretches higher up where those same people seldom go. One thing I try to remember is that, as tempting as it is, you can't necessarily judge the quality of a trout stream by the amount of water it carries. (That's assuming, of course, that it carries some and that it flows year-round.) Remember that if you take a foot-deep stream and dig a ten-foot-deep hole in it, the flow will stay the same, but that hole will still fill with water.

All it takes is a meadow with some undercut banks, or maybe a section of pocket water with some deep plunge pools, or a series of logjams that back the stream up. Things like this seldom show themselves on maps—except for the paper napkin variety—but there can be some clues. On topographic maps, I always look for places where the contour lines show level spots in otherwise steep country. "Ah ha!" I think, "the hidden meadow." Tight contour lines bending along the blue line of the creek mean a canyon, which in turn means pocket water, not to mention tough hiking.

Beaver ponds can make all the difference in the world, and they do show up on good topographic maps, but that can be misleading. As I said, beaver ponds can have fairly short life spans as good fisheries, and many of the ones shown on my USGS maps are long since silted in or blown out.

I remember the very day I learned that. I found a string of ponds on the map not far from here and dashed up there to fish them, only to find them nearly reverted back to meadow. I wasn't exactly disappointed—I had a good hike and caught some trout in the stream—but I did get the map out again. Sure enough, down in the lower left-hand corner it said "from aerial photographs taken in 1954, field checked 1960." I could only wonder how good the ponds had been eighteen years ago when the map was new.

The best beaver ponds I currently know of are not on my maps because they're too fresh. Or, I should say, they *are* on the maps, but only because I've drawn them in myself. Maybe I should stop doing that. A map could fall into the wrong hands.

I still like to check ponds out, though, because there are sometimes new ones in the vicinity of old ones and now and then one will last for a long, long time, either because it's especially large to begin with or it's in an area where neither silt nor the high runoffs that blow out dams are a problem. Based on some experience and many stories, my impression is that beaver ponds last longer in flat country than in the mountains.

The quality of fishing in a beaver pond can sometimes depend on the kind of trout you're dealing with, too. A pond filled with something like cutthroats or rainbows will likely have decent fish in it for as long as the habitat remains viable, but brook trout tend to overpopulate a pond and then stunt because there isn't enough food to go around, so even if the pond lasts for a good, long time, the fishing can peter off in a few seasons.

On the other hand, a pond can grow some very large brook trout in its early years: big, fat, deep-bellied, brilliantly colored beaver-pond brookies that are worth any amount of walking, and even some wasted trips, to get into.

As sad as it is to see a good beaver pond go downhill, it's just that wonderful to catch one at its height. Not only can you take some big trout, but you can congratulate yourself on your exquisite sense of timing.

Hatches

There are other areas where timing is important, like hatches, for instance. A good hatch or fall of insects is the supreme event in fly fishing, the one thing that can make an otherwise stubborn trout stream spill its guts, revealing sizes and numbers of fish you never dreamed were there.

Small-stream hatches can be puzzling because you often won't know when they're going to come off or even what bugs will be involved. That, in fact, is why I've come to depend on a relative handful of general patterns for small-stream fishing. Even if I wanted to match the hatch—an approach I have nothing against—I wouldn't know where to start in most cases. As I said in the chapter on flies, it's a good idea to hedge your bets by carrying patterns that copy locally common hatches and maybe even the regional favorite attractor fly. Beyond that, a lot of it is guesswork.

I'd like to present a formula here for timing the small-stream hatches to the ones on the main river that everyone who fishes knows about, even if they call it by the wrong name. The best I can do is offer a few observations that might help.

With early-season hatches that are known to move upstream, you'll often find that the bugs appear later up in the tributaries than they do down on the river. If

I had to guess, I'd say that's a function of water temperature, which tends to warm up more slowly in the
headwaters. Midseason hatches, like caddisflies, will
sometimes come off at about the same time, while fall-
hatching bugs seem to want to emerge either at the
same time, or maybe a bit earlier, than their counter-
parts in the river.

That's not a rule of thumb because I couldn't swear
that it will pan out even half the time. Let's just say it's
something to mull over if you like to do a little mulling
before you wet a line. I guess the real piece of advice
hiding in here is, if everyone on the river is catching
fish on a #14 Red Quill, take some of those with you
when you go up one of the creeks.

Another situation you'll encounter is where the
streams have different bugs in them than the rivers and
lakes. This seems most likely to happen when the habitat types are noticeably different, say, fast, cool creeks
emptying into slower, somewhat warmer rivers. Bottom
structure also makes a difference here. If the river has
a silty bottom, there may be lots of those big burrowing mayfly nymphs in it, but if the creeks are rocky-
bottomed, the predominant mayflies will probably be
clingers.

By the same token, on a drainage in flat terrain where
you have a slow river fed by equally slow feeder creeks
running off the same kind of country, you can sometimes fish the same hatch for twenty miles in both
directions.

Of course, advice from the local expert can be a big
help, even if it's vague. Knowing that the Pale Morning
Duns usually come off "sometime in June or early
July" is better than knowing nothing at all. Even if you
have only a hint as to what insects produce the major

hatches, you can sometimes cross-reference that with some of the fly-fishing entomology books that give general hatch dates for different parts of the country. This can be vague, too, but, once again, it's better than nothing.

Spawning Runs

A spawning run is another event that can really turn a small stream around. Even in a spawning run that's comprised of nothing but resident creek trout, you'll often spot fish that are larger than you thought were in there. These are the ones that live quiet lives in deep holes or undercut banks, but who, when they feel that old black magic, lose all caution and sense of decorum.

Maybe something like that has happened to you at one time or another.

The trout in lakes and reservoirs invariably run up the feeder streams to spawn, and here again we're talking about the possibility of some really big fish.

Spawning runs are very difficult to time correctly. Knowing that browns and brookies spawn in the fall, while rainbows, cutts, and goldens do it in the spring, is the starting point, but it will vary from stream to stream and from season to season. A biologist told me recently that spawning times are determined by season, water temperature, and length of daylight, but he wasn't prepared to say which factor took precedence.

I know from experience that the brown trout in the stream across the street usually begin to show up on the spawning beds sometime in November, while the same species farther up the drainage will do it as much as a month earlier. I know, also, that when the browns at a given altitude are spawning, there's a fair chance that the brookies in that neighborhood are moving as

In lake country, look for small streams connecting good trout lakes.

well, although there's no guarantee of that. Some years it's seemed as though half the trout in the county woke up horny on the same day, while in other seasons the beginning and ending dates for the spawning runs wouldn't be the same for any two creeks.

In the cutthroat lakes at the higher altitudes, spring can come late and the cutts will sometimes be running out of the lakes as late as July. Altitude has a lot to do with all this, I think. Way up high where summers are maddeningly short, I've seen spring-spawning cutthroats and fall-spawning brookies on the beds at the same time.

How far up a stream will spawning trout go? Apparently, as far as they have to before they come to the first stretch of pea-sized gravel. If that's ten feet from the lake, fine. If it's a mile or two, that seems to be fine also.

In some parts of the country spawning runs are followed avidly. Around here the style seems to be to try to stumble upon them. That is, you fish often in what should be the season, and you carry some brightly colored streamers. Sooner or later you hit it, and in between times you get in some fine fall dry-fly fishing.

Casting to spawning trout is a little different than what most of us are used to. The idea isn't to fool the fish into eating something that looks like food because he's not too hungry at the moment. You're trying to make him mad or, if you prefer, to "trigger a territorial response." That's why streamers are so good; they're seen as little fish who are being pests either by invading the trout's space or trying to steal the eggs.

This kind of thing takes patience: many casts, many drifts, many swings right past the nose of the trout you want. It's a teasing kind of fishing and takes some time. Sometimes you don't catch them, but they're usually big enough that it's well worth trying. In November, several years ago, on his birthday, I watched A. K. catch a twenty-two-inch brown from a stream no wider than a parking space.

Later, sitting in the truck drinking coffee from a thermos, we debated about where this fish had come from. Maybe he was a resident small-stream trout who had grown fat on a diet of little brookies, of which there were plenty. That's more likely than many people think, especially in the case of those notoriously carnivorous browns. Then again, maybe he was a spawner from the reservoir downstream, although if that was true it would have involved a rugged four-mile swim.

It ended as these discussions often do: we decided that we'd never know for sure and probably didn't even care all that much. It's just that a trout of that size from a little creek needs to be talked about for a while.

You'll sometimes see trout running out of a river into a tributary stream to spawn, but this seems to be less common than in the case of lakes and reservoirs. That's because there are usually some good spawning areas in the river itself and, just as a trout will go as far as he has to to get the business taken care of, he also won't go any farther than necessary. Still, it does happen, and if you're out on the river in what should be spawning season, it wouldn't hurt to investigate the creeks a little.

Runoff and Weather

And there are other seasonal considerations on small streams. In some parts of the country the spring runoff is enough to drive fly fishermen bats. Here's the warm weather after a long winter; the trees are budding, the birds are singing, and the trout streams are muddy. This is when you can sit around the fly shop all afternoon drinking stale coffee and listening to your colleagues bitch. "We had a lot of snow last winter," someone says, and after an appropriate silence, someone else adds, "Yup, rivers could be muddy for a month yet."

The rivers, yes, but maybe not the small streams. They carry less water, even in the spring flood, and they drain less countryside, which means they drop and clear sooner.

Bitch sessions at the fly shop are a rite of spring and you are required to take part in them, but once you've put in your appearance, it's fun to go out and catch a few trout from the feeder creeks, just to break up the monotony.

Of course, it doesn't always work (nothing I've said here *always* works) and there have been spring days when friends and I hiked miles without getting past the roily water. At least until you have it figured out, it's probably best to do it by car, going from one bridge or access point to the next—always working upstream—until you find clear water.

If you don't find clear water, you can go back to the fly shop and say, "Well, boys, it's even worse than we thought."

The way weather affects the fishing is something else you can debate endlessly at the fly shop. Some weird things will come up, like subtle changes in water chemistry, variations in oxygenation due to the photosynthesis of aquatic plants, barometric pressure, phases of the moon, and such. One thing I've noticed, though, is that things like this are not used so much to predict the quality of the fishing as to make the excuses offered afterward sound more scientific.

With that in mind, here's what I think about weather and small streams: The best thing you can hope for is a cool, damp, cloudy day. Trout are negatively photo-tropic, which is what a biologist will say when he means they aren't fond of direct sunlight. Fishermen believe that, to a trout, shade or darkness means cover; it's what makes the fish feel safe and, therefore, a little more casual about moving around to feed.

I believe that to be true everywhere, but it's especially helpful on small streams where cover is at a minimum and the fish are skittish.

Bugs, most notably the mayflies, also seem to like cloudy days and will often hatch for longer periods of time and in greater numbers when it's overcast. If it also happens to be a little cooler or damper than usual, the bugs will stay on the water longer, probably be-cause it takes more time for their freshly emerged wings to dry.

On those glorious days when all that comes together, you can have a heavy mayfly hatch fed upon eagerly by confident trout. A light breeze can help by ruffling the surface of the water, which can make the trout feel even safer and also help to cover your approach and cast. A gusty intermittent wind can blow a lot of terrestrials into the water, producing a rise even without a legiti-mate hatch. The best is the one that blows across a meadow full of grasshoppers in late summer.

A thin drizzle can enhance a cloudy day by, again, ruffling the surface of the stream, and also by dampen-ing the wings of freshly hatched bugs.

As with other aspects of life, too much of a good thing can turn bad. If the breeze turns to a gale, you can't cast. If the drizzle turns to a heavy rain, it can cancel the hatch and put the fish down. A cold rain on an already cool stream can lower water temperatures more than the fish like. It can also raise the stream level and muddy the water.

Then again, if it's high summer and the stream is a little too warm, a nice rain can cool it down and wake up the trout. A quick rain that comes and goes in fifteen minutes may have knocked hundreds of bugs out of the air and off of the banks to produce, for a short time after it's over, a fabulous this-and-that hatch.

A slug of slightly off-colored current running down each bank after a short heavy rain might contain all sorts of beetles, ants, and worms that trout will eat. Run a big nymph through there and see what happens. If that same short cloudburst raises the whole level of the stream, run a weighted nymph through the deeper pockets. The stronger current may have flushed all kinds of nymphs into the flow and the trout could be feeding furiously down there. If the water has turned cloudy, use a big dark nymph that the fish will be able to see.

I guess what all this boils down to is, things are magnified on small streams; a little breeze or squall that would pass over a river almost unnoticed can have a profound effect on the little creek that feeds it. Whatever happens with the weather can bode well or ill depending on, well, depending on things you'll only be able to figure out after the fact, if at all.

"The wind came up, the hatch ended, and we never caught another fish all day."

"The wind came up, covered the water with grasshoppers, and we caught fish all afternoon."

Whatever happens, you might as well keep fishing. I mean, you're a fisherman and there you are on the stream. You're not gonna go home are you?